GENDER

Key Concepts in Philosophy

Key Concepts in Philosophy
Series Editors: John Mullarkey (University of Dundee) and
Caroline Williams (Queen Mary, University of London)

Gender

Key Concepts in Philosophy

Tina Chanter

continuum

Continuum International Publishing Group   80 Maiden Lane
The Tower Building   Suite 704
11 York Road   New York
London SE1 7NX   NY 10038

© Tina Chanter 2006

British Library Cataloguing-in-Publication Data
A catalogue record for this book is available from the British Library.

ISBN: HB: 0-8264-7168-4
9780826471680
PB: 0-8264-7169-2
9780826471697

Library of Congress Cataloging-in-Publication Data
Chanter, Tina, 1960–
    Gender : key concepts in philosophy / Tina Chanter.
    p.   cm.
    Includes bibliographical references.
    ISBN-13: 978-0-8264-7168-0
    ISBN-10: 0-8264-7168-4
    ISBN-13: 978-0-8264-7169-7 (pbk.)
    ISBN-10: 0-8264-7169-2 (pbk.)
    1. Feminist theory. 2. Sex role. 3. Gender identity. I. Title.
HQ1190.C46   2007
305.4201–dc22

2006024031

Typeset by Servis Filmsetting Ltd, Manchester
Printed and bound in Great Britain by
MPG Books Ltd, Bodmin, Cornwall

CONTENTS

THE CHALLENGE OF TRANSGENDERED IDENTITY: THE END OF GENDER AS WE KNOW IT?

It was only a matter of time. We have heard about the death of God and the end of metaphysics; now the end of gender has been announced. These are interesting and difficult times for gender theorists. Science fiction scenarios, in which people morph from male to female in the blink of an eye, have become all too familiar. The line between fiction and reality seems to be increasingly fuzzy, now that we can present ourselves as whatever gender we want through Internet personas. The proliferation of gender identity clinics, which enable female to male and male to female operations, also suggests that sex/gender is much more malleable than we might have once thought. Even the procedures of in-vitro fertilization have rendered unstable what used to be a central, defining feature of what it meant to be a woman or a man. With the increase in test-tube babies and frozen-sperm banks, reproductive processes are no longer what they were. You don't need to be a heterosexual couple to produce babies any more. All you need is lots of money, lots of patience, and lots of luck. Designer babies are highly sought after, in the form of long-legged, athletic, blonde, Harvard-educated egg-donors. Lesbian couples and single women are having babies, gay male couples can have babies with the help of surrogate mothers. Sex isn't what it used to be – and neither, it would seem, is gender.

Transgendered identities, including intersexuality, transsexuality, and other crossover terms, are challenging tried and trusted feminist formulae, which equate gender with society (or culture, or history) and sex with biology (or physiology, or nature). Some transsexuals opt for surgical procedures so that they become anatomically the opposite sex, and some do not. Those who opt for and have had gender reassignment surgery are post-operative transsexuals, and those who want it and plan to have it are pre-operative. There are also transsexuals who opt to live as a man or a woman, without getting breast implants or penile surgery (depending on the direction of the transition, f to m or m to f), who either do not want or cannot have surgery. Taking hormones can reduce body hair, affect the voice, and change body shape. It can also cause medical complications, so that after taking hormones, for some individuals, surgery is not an option. Transsexuals can live as the sex with which they identify by wearing feminine or masculine clothes, for example. A transsexual who identifies as a woman could still have a penis, but could look like, act like, and want to be a woman. She identifies as such, lives as such, and passes as such. To such a woman, it is important to be identified by the gender with which she identifies, and wants to pass as. Counsellors report that most transsexuals have identified with the opposite sex from a very young age.

How does all this impact theories about gender? Does the apparent extreme fluidity of gender roles confirm or disprove postmodern theories of gender? Has postmodernism rejected if not biological, then psychic determinism, prematurely? Or is it rather that those who reject postmodernism out of hand have failed to understand that, far from offering a deterministic social constructionist account of bodies or materiality, postmodernism in fact embraces a more nuanced account of gender? Feminist theorists have got quite a lot of mileage out of the sex/gender distinction, to say the least. Does the transgendered age herald the end of gender as we know it? Is it, after all, impossible to distinguish sex (bodies, physiognomy, anatomy) from gender (social or cultural norms that dictate how femininity and masculinity are construed)? Does gender precede sex, as some feminist theorists have put it? Does gender go all the way down, as it were? Or does transgender experience give the lie to such claims? Is there, after all, some incorporeal reality to gender, which is neither reducible to anatomy, nor to social, cultural or political norms? If transgendered individuals know their true gender, irrespective both of their bodies and/or the gendered messages to which they have been exposed since childbirth, does this suggest that there is some third factor that explains femininity or masculinity which is irreducible to both the domains that have been named sex and gender?

In philosophy, immense amounts of energy are spent trying to get away from some key historical presuppositions. Back in the day, Cartesian mind–body dualism set the terms not just for thinking about how we know what we know – epistemological claims about the world – but also (albeit inadvertently and circuitously) how feminist theory constructs its view of gender. A founding distinction of modern philosophy, Descartes' separation of mind and body has come to inform the assumption that there is an inner essence or truth of gender of which the body is an expression. Contrary to this dualistic model, good postmodernists that we are, we have learned that there is no Cartesian-style inner essence of gender (mind/spirit) that the body expresses, rather there is only a series of performative acts which signify and resignify gender. Gender is not something that is 'inside,' a pre-existent essence, waiting to find bodily expression. There is no inner truth awaiting 'authentic' or 'proper' realization in bodily or material acts. Gender is always already lived, gestural, corporeal, culturally mediated and historically constituted. It is not that we have a core, essential, unambiguous femininity or masculinity struggling to get out, or to find appropriate expression. Rather, there are cultural dictates, according to which subjects construct themselves, by appropriating and sometimes reinventing or subverting historically situated gender codes. As soon as we are born (perhaps even before) we are color coded as boy or girl, and systematically trained according to our genders. Our rooms are painted sky blue and decorated with mobiles of toy planes, or rose pink and decorated with flowers. We are either given barbie dolls to play with and dressed in frilly clothes, or footballs to kick around and pants to wear.

To be sure, we are born with certain genitalia, according to which our expected genders are read. Expectations are formed, cultural ideologies are imbibed, and it is expected that those who are identified as anatomical girls will act like girls, while those who are identified as anatomical boys act like boys. As we have already begun to see, a number of complicating factors come into the picture, however. The more transgendered identity comes to the fore, the more we discover that cultural expectations have led to early surgical intervention to ensure that individuals accord with our ideas of gender. Intersexed, or ambiguously sexed, infants have been subject to operations to bring them into line with conventional ideas about female and male identity. Hermaphroditism, as it used to be called, is hardly new. Parents have had to make difficult decisions about how to respond to intersexed infants, decisions that have been made in the attempt to make their lives viable. In some cases, such infants have been brought up as one sex, after having undergone surgery to eliminate anatomical ambiguity, but feel that their assigned sex does not accord with what they feel themselves to be. Even infants who are understood to have no knowledge of surgical intervention (who have undergone surgery before they were able to verbally communicate) experience a misfit between their assigned gender and their actual gender. Transsexuals also experience a disconnect between body and their gender. It might seem then, that even if there is no inner truth to gender in the Cartesian sense, neither is gender wholly culturally contingent on social interaction, that it cannot be accounted for entirely as a social production. If gender is not merely a matter of cultural conditioning, there might be, after all, if not some innate, biological influence, then at least something ineffable about gender. Yet how far the ineffability of gender can be attributed to any natural or genetic claims remains in question, given that all of us, without exception, are born into a world replete with gender norms to which we find ourselves subject. These norms pre-exist us, and we react to them, negotiating a world that includes gendered expectations well before we learn to code that negotiation in speech. How far transgenderism demands a reworking of the idea that gender is an ongoing production or performance, which is enacted in an intersubjective world and structured by stereotypical gendered assumptions, remains, then, an open question. The jury is still out on this.

Alain Berliner's 1997 *Ma vie en rose* (My life in pink), a Belgian film which deals with the question of transsexuality in a sensitive and intelligent way, has a lighthearted, whimsical touch. Seven-year-old Ludovic has no doubt that he wants to be a girl. Ludovic's identification is clear enough, but his family, schoolmates, and the parents of his schoolmates are less than sanguine about his decision. He is asked to leave his school, his father loses his job, and his family is forced out of the middle-class neighborhood into which it has recently moved. Realizing that he is causing his family all sorts of problems simply by trying to be who he is, Ludovic climbs into a freezer, narrowly avoiding suicide when his frantic mother finds him. Ludovic's experience is not unusual. A high percentage of transgendered individuals attempt suicide at some point in their lives, and some succeed. Transgenderism is not, it is clear, something that is undertaken lightly, or without penalty. Ludovic's character enables us to see that, far from being some monstrous, unnatural, anomaly, he is merely an innocent child, who cannot understand why his parents, siblings, and schoolmates find it so difficult to simply allow him to be who he wants to be. He identifies as a girl, he wants to wear dresses and look pretty, he wants to play Snow White in the school play, and he wants to marry Jerome. He rationalizes the situation by explaining that God must have made a mistake when he was handing out the chromosomes. His X chromosome must have fallen down the chimney. He escapes from the gendered strictures that confront him at every turn by taking off in flights of fantasy with Pam and Ben (the continental equivalent of Ken and Barbie). We join him on some of these fantasies, as does Ludovic's mother at one point, when she climbs up a ladder to a billboard, in pursuit of Ludovic, and enters into the world of fantasy Ludovic has invented, drawing on popular culture, in order to cope with a world that construes his sexuality as deviant and aberrant.

Conceding that any account we might provide of the physical or 'natural' aspects of existence is going to be necessarily ideologically loaded, postmodernism offers the insight that there is no straightforward causal model between sex and gender. Indeed, some feminist theorists have argued that rather than posit a causal relation between sex and gender, we reverse the causal reasoning, to claim instead that gender precedes sex Such an argument appeals to the importance of having separated off gender from sex in the first place, thereby establishing a 'strategic location' from which to challenge the idea that sex is stable, unchanging or fixed. As Christine Delphy (1993) asks, when we posit the distinction between sex and gender are we comparing something natural with something social or something social that also turns out to be social? Once it is determined that at least part of what used to go under the label of sex can be redefined as gender, a space is opened up from which to argue that the entire domain of sex or biology is in fact subject to interpretation. Our ideas of biology emanate from certain culturally specific and historically discrete, prescriptive conceptions of gender, the normative force of which derives from the discourse of biology, which is itself subject to hegemonic forces. The 'truth' about our bodies will turn out to be reflective of certain cultural biases, including the idea that naturalistic explanations can best account for social phenomena. The very conception of bodies as harboring a material causality that is easily or readily distinguishable from societal influences implies that there is some part of 'nature' that is outside 'society.' Yet the suggestion that some natural ground that we designate 'sex' both pre-exists and causes 'gender' assumes both that nature somehow stands outside our interpretation of it, and that it precedes or comes before any interpretation. On this view, any idea that we have of gender will be consequent on the inherent nature of sex. On the other hand, to hold to a consistent position, social constructionists must do away with the idea that sex comes first, that it logically and chronologically precedes any interpretation of it. Rather, all we have are various competing interpretations of sex, all of which derive from a series of commitments that are ultimately political in nature. There is no metaphysical or ontological precedence that dictates ideologies of gender. Ideological constructs arise, gain prevalence and legitimacy, and come to appear natural. Sex then comes to represent, after the fact, the 'ground' of gender, yet its foundational role is one that derives from a social consensus about what sex should be.

The idealized and naturalized status of biological claims is to be attributed, then, not to any innate characteristics, but precisely to the process by which dominant views gain currency and come to seem natural and beyond question. This process of naturalization or normalization, whereby the very terms available for thinking about the relation between sex and gender are terms which confirm the interests of dominant groups, has as its byproduct the de-legitimation of any views that would present a challenge to the status quo. Rather than occurring as a contested term, sex appears to exert authority over gender. Sex is read as if embedded within it were certain inherent meanings, meanings which in fact derive from ideological interpretations of what sex should be. Sex, as Delphy (1993) suggests, is itself a 'sign' – its status is 'symbolic.' Certain bodies come to be marked as female, and others come to be marked as male. While borrowing the trappings of gender, sex is envisaged as if its significance were always already in place, inscribed in nature, as it were. To argue that there are 'naturally' two and only two sexes, male and female, and that the traits of these sexes are mutually exclusive, is to mirror the heterosexist beliefs of the dominant, western, advanced, late-capitalist era, and to construe the function of sex to be teleologically circumscribed by the end of reproduction. It is to ignore the many cultures in which gender is not dependent on some bodily trait, but is precisely variable (see Guerrero 1997). It is to ignore that whatever content we read into what we call sex is going to be significantly weighted according to culturally prescriptive beliefs about gender, so that it will be all but impossible to separate out normative dimensions of gender from our 'biological' or 'scientific' ideas about sex.

Science itself is ideologically driven: there is no purely scientific definition of male and female, only culturally circumscribed interpretations of data that give rise to certain views, some of which come to form part of the 'scientific' canon. This canon itself is far from immune from assumptions deriving from its practitioners, most of whom, up until fairly recently, have been white, privileged, western, and male, and many of whom are still dominated by patriarchal, white, bourgeois assumptions. Unsurprisingly, then, those accounts that have been able to accumulate institutional authority have tended to reflect the prejudices of traditional, cultural beliefs, which in patriarchal, heterosexist, Judeo-Christian societies has meant that prevailing ideas about the oppositional categories of gender have held sway. Accordingly, the mutually exclusive binary opposition between male and female has acquired a normative force that has all but outlawed sexualities that do not neatly adhere to such a theoretical commitment. What often still remains obscured is the fact that such commitments are ideologically driven, as is the science that assumes them and then provides confirmation of them, engaging in a circularity that does not open itself up to challenge.

CHAPTER 1

FORMATIVE MOMENTS AND CONCEPTS IN THE HISTORY OF FEMINISM

Feminist theorists have put a good deal of energy into trying to combat traditional gender ideologies and to overcome naturalizing claims about women's innate inferiority to men or female irrationality. Even as we point out the limiting role it has played in some circles, we must also acknowledge that the distinction between sex and gender has served the feminist movement well. It has played a crucial role in establishing parity in the workplace, for example. Once the idea that women are innately incapable of reasoning well, or naturally unsuited to the rigors of public life, is put to rest, it quickly becomes clear that what stands in the way of women's progress is convention, tradition, or opinion, rather than nature, biology, or physiology.

Early feminist arguments focused upon the unfairness of the fact that women were excluded from some central activities crucial to humanity – the defining activities of modern political identity – which men appeared to be granted by natural fiat. These included the right to take an active role in politics, government, and leadership; the right to political representation; the right to education; the right to self-definition; the right to legal ownership, and the right to bequeath an inheritance. Arguably, then, the modern feminist movement began as a movement that tried to establish parity with men.

There are however a number of reasons to be wary of defining feminism as a movement to achieve equality. If we assume that feminism aims to accomplish the equality of women with men, the question arises, which men? With whom do women want equality? Presumably feminists are not striving to be the equals of oppressed, disenfranchised, or disadvantaged men. It becomes clear then that an inexplicit assumption built into the idea that feminists should strive for equality with men is that women seek equality with privileged men. Since privilege plays itself out in ways that typically benefit white, middle class, and heterosexual identities, to define feminism in terms of equality is in effect to build into the definition of feminism privileged assumptions that bias it from the start. Accordingly, bell hooks argues that feminism should be defined not as a movement for equality, but as a struggle against oppression, one which acknowledges that oppression is not confined to sexism, but is also expressed in classism, racism, and heterosexism. By challenging oppression on multiple fronts, hooks avoids assuming that all women share a similar relationship to class, race, and sexuality. Rather than perpetuating what has been dubbed the 'invisibility of whiteness,' hooks calls for an inter-relational model of gender, race, class, and sexuality, and advocates a coalitional understanding of feminism. This avoids positing gender as the foundational or grounding concept, while tacitly treating race, class, and sexuality as peripheral or derivative categories, whose importance can only ever be secondary to gender. Such a model presents gender as if it were a neutral term with regard to race, class, and sexuality, as if it applied universally to all women, while covertly interpreting gender according to the norm (white, middle class, and heterosexual).

In 1949 in *The Second Sex* Simone de Beauvoir pointed out that maleness is understood to be the norm – as neutral or universal. It would not occur to men to write a book about their situation or point of view, precisely because such a point of view is, by default, taken to be the universal position. To explain the human condition is to explain, by and large, what is in fact a masculine position. By contrast, it occurs to women to write about their situation because of the asymmetrical relationship between the sexes. Woman is, as Beauvoir famously suggested, the Other, the inessential, while man is the absolute, the subject, the essential. Women are understood as relative to men – as the other of men, as less than, or inferior to men.

Wary of embracing concepts such as equality as the goal of feminism, since the vagueness of the term lent itself to bad faith, allowing men to formally acknowledge women's equality while refusing women as equals when it came to substantive issues, Beauvoir formulated instead a feminist philosophy based on that of existentialist ethics. As radically free, we are all subjects, capable of defining our destinies, transcending whatever obstacles confront us, and realizing our potential freedom. By the same token, as free, we are all subject to the temptation to forgo our freedom, to deny our liberty, or to act in the mode of being-in-itself (*être-en-soi*). Sometimes it is less challenging to take the easy route, to allow someone else to decide on our behalves. Women have been tempted to allow men to make the important ethical decisions on their behalf. To do so is to eschew responsibility for their own lives. If we refuse to take responsibility for our freedom, preferring to acquiesce to the will of someone else, choosing to give up being the authors of our own lives, we condemn ourselves to the status of things. We act as if we have no choice other than to be what we have become. If, on the other hand, we suffer from oppression, the failure to realize our freedom is not a moral fault, but rather a matter of being compelled to assume the position of subjects who are not recognized in their subjectivity. Beauvoir, then, was critical of women for being complicit with their own oppression, while at the same time critical of men for continuing to occupy the role of oppressors. She argues that men have typically denied their corporeality, and that women have typically taken responsibility for men's embodiment.

In the light of feminist theorists who insist on an intersectional model of race, class, sexuality, and gender, Beauvoir's point about the conflation of universality with masculinity can be extended to race, class, and sexuality. Just as the masculine position is assumed to be universal, applicable to all humanity, while in fact harboring a specificity that privileges masculinity over femininity, so feminism, unless it is vigilant about addressing the diversity among women, is liable to reiterate a false universalism. The category of 'women' operates as if it were blind to race, yet persistently betrays a racial bias towards the invisibly privileged category of whiteness. Similarly, the category of 'blacks' operates as if it were gender-blind, yet consistently privileges masculinity over femininity. The title of the 1980s collection *All the Women are White, all the Blacks are Men, but Some of Us are Brave* (Hull et al. 1982) expresses the problem succinctly. Feminism defines itself, by default, as invisibly white, while race theorists define the issues, by default, as invisibly masculine. Black women are caught in the middle, implicitly asked to justify their existence as black by feminism, and to justify their existence as women by race theory. Once again, a false universalism rears its ugly head. Caught between a rock and hard place, African-American feminists have had to fight hard to establish their concerns as legitimate on two fronts.

It is not enough then to adopt an additive model. To do so is to envisage race, gender, class, and sexuality as if they were separable strands or segments of social life that develop independently of one another, which can be added together, or subtracted from one another, as if they had integrity in and of themselves. This fails to account for the fact that subjects do not experience race, gender, class, or sexuality as separate axes, easily separable or quantifiable dimensions of experience. hooks points out the importance of avoiding what she calls the 'competitive' or 'either/or' thinking embedded in the assumption that being a woman or being African-American can be played off against one another in an attempt to ascertain which aspect of identity is more important. It further fails to acknowledge the extent to which even well-intentioned, but still misguided, attempts to be inclusive of difference try to add on factors such as race, class, and sexuality to analyses that still assume gender as foundational (hooks 1984), without changing the whole picture. Spelman (1988) points out that additive models often still trade in privilege.

We need to acknowledge that the very categories of race, class, gender, and sexuality are abstract, analytic categories of analysis that by definition only tend to capture those synchronic, structural features of experience that lend themselves readily to formalization. In fact, the experience of race, class, and gender is shaped by myriad, incalculable, historically specific details which can never be captured by the analytic categories of race, class, and gender without reducing their specificity. This does not mean we should simply get rid of these categories, as some theorists have advised in the case of race, but it does mean that we need to exercise extreme caution in order not to overlook the fact that each of these categories of analysis tends to oversimplify a complex field of phenomena, that each of them is indebted to quite specific historical developments, and that each of them came to light at particular historical moments, in ways that are culturally loaded. The disciplinary assumptions of 1960s psychology and sociology, along with the demography of the feminist movement, have helped to inflect the term gender, for example, in particular ways. Prior to the 1970s, when the term 'gender' gained currency, in the wake of Margaret Mead's anthropological work, the concept of 'sex roles' was prominent. Indebted to Mead, but also deriving from sociology, which inflected it in a Parsonian direction, the idea of a role expressed the active aspect of one's status, and so was defined according to work performed within a social setting. As one's status changes, so does one's role, or social function. The idea of sex roles, or what later came to be called gender, acknowledged that one's identity was not determined from birth, according to some intrinsic nature, but rather was dependent upon the structural roles individuals played in society. Such roles are developed in relation to social structures, which change over time, and can be multiple (worker, friend, and mother, for example). The variability of gender, as opposed to what Ann Oakley identified as the 'constancy' of sex, is what made gender so central to the feminist program.

If the concept of gender was inherited from anthropology and filtered through sociological and psychological lenses, the concept of race first arose in the contexts of various systems of classification. It has been argued that the birth of the modern concept of race is bound up with the history of slavery and colonization, while the concept of class cannot, of course, be abstracted from the history of industrial capitalism. Each term carries the baggage of having become a rallying point for oppression, but none of them have developed in isolation from one another, and none of them are transparent concepts. Each carries with it a complex history, histories which reveal profound tensions and conflicts between the social movements that built up around these concepts. If mainstream feminism has enlisted gender in ways that have been race-blind, race theorists have enlisted race in ways that have perpetuated gender-blindness. This suggests that in order to confront the complex histories in which gender, race, sexuality, and class have been implicated in one another, we have to be responsible for acknowledging that each concept has been played out in negative ways in the configuration of the others. If gender has been race-blind, enlightened versions of feminism cannot merely be content to add race to gender, for example, since race has always been implicated in gender theorizing, albeit in invisible ways. It must therefore be a question of first rendering visible the exclusionary models of race that have contributed to prevailing models of gender, and then providing more adequate models of race. Rather than race being a marker of women who are considered to deviate from an invisibly white norm, the invisible whiteness of the category 'gender' must be made to account for itself. Even the language of visibility is inadequate since to render visible that which was previously invisible is not enough. It is necessary to articulate this new-found visibility in ways that challenge the terms dictating who is allowed to become visible and what standards determine that visibility.

THE IMPORTANCE OF WOMEN'S RIGHT TO VOTE

Perhaps the most momentous change for women in the history of women's rights was the achievement of the franchise, which did not come about until the twentieth century. Ever since the suffragettes, who chained themselves to the railings of parliament in protest against their denial of the vote, feminists have worked hard to build on the right to vote, still not secured in some countries. Other crucial rights included that of legal recognition as property owners – the right to own property in one's own name, and the right to be able to confer that property on one's children – and the right to gain entry into university. Virginia Woolf's imaginative tour de force, *Orlando* (1956), part biography, part novel, and part political satire, comments on the irony that the fact of being a woman prevents Orlando from his/her inheritance. When Orlando wakes up, after a long sleep, only to find that he has turned into a woman, she quickly discovers that her inexplicable sex change prohibits her from owning the property that was his by right as a man. Woolf's suggestion is that this state of affairs is equally inexplicable. Inspired by Woolf's prescient fantasy, Sally Potter's 1992 film *Orlando*, like Woolf's novel, not only wreaks havoc with our sedimented ideas about gender, but also indulges in time-travel, spanning a number of centuries. We witness a marriage proposal to Orlando, in which it is pointed out that, now she is a woman, she is, from a legal point of view, as good as dead. By the end of the film, Orlando, who by now has a son, has donned the leathers of a motorcycle rider.

Contrary to various models found throughout the history of philosophy which posit women as inferior to men (including those of Aristotle and Freud, who both in different ways regard women as deficient men), feminists argued that women are not determined by any innate inferiority. Women were only considered unsuited to the roles reserved for men because they lacked the education to be politically informed, responsible citizens. Once given this opportunity, there was no reason why women could not be just as good as men. The form that this argument often took was that there was nothing about women's physical nature, nothing about female bodies or reproductive capacities, that prevented women from succeeding in the public or political realm, as well as in the private or domestic realm. The fact that women have reproductive capacities has no bearing upon their ability to be good at public policy. It is worth noting that this was in fact a recapitulation of the kind of arguments Plato had used in the *Republic* to make the point that there was no reason why women could not be guardians or philosopher kings of his ideal city (Plato 1978). Plato has Socrates argue that the fact that some men are different from others in some respects – for example some men are bald, while others have hair – has no bearing on their capacity to rule. Similarly, women's reproductive capacities should not preclude them from government. The fact that women have wombs and can give birth has nothing to do with their ability to play active roles in the political realm. Although Plato was not feminist in the sense that we tend to use the term feminism in contemporary times – as a term referring to women's oppression or rights – the fact that he anticipated early feminist arguments about sameness remains significant. Plato did not, however, see fit to extend his arguments to all social echelons of his ideal city. His arguments applied only to the wives of the male guardians, that is, only to the ruling class of the city that Plato has Socrates paint in words.

The arguments that Plato and early feminist thinkers made amounted to the idea that it was not women's sexual identity – not their bodies, their sex, their reproductive capacities – that determined their natures, but convention, society, habit, or tradition. This is a version of the nature/nurture argument. Nature does not dictate whether women should be confined to motherhood, nurture does. The crucial shift that occurs here is that women's identity is not fixed by destiny, anatomy, genes, biology, or DNA. Rather it is capable of change, fluid and malleable. Once it is admitted that women's physical, material, biological nature does not determine them, but social trends, customs, beliefs, and prejudices limit and prescribe their roles, then the door is opened for re-education, transformation, and social change. Feminists rejected the idea that women are ruled by emotion, illogical, the weaker sex, slaves of fashion, given to envy (Freud), jealousy, vanity, and pettiness (Rousseau); in short that we are in need of the protection of men, who are stronger not only physically but also mentally, more competent, and more reliable than women, whose frailty, flightiness, and inconstancy is stressed. Instead women strove for independence, and in doing so, sought to combat the mythical belief that women are ruled by emotions, subject to irrationality and incapable of self-government, let alone the government of others.

The traditional view that women's place was in the home was based, usually, on some claim that women were naturally or constitutionally unfit to take part in the public or political domain, which was there-fore marked as masculine. Women were seen as innately, inherently incompetent when it came to political affairs. Mary Wollstonecraft pointed to the implicit contradiction in this position in *A Vindication of the Rights of Women* (1791). On the one hand women were seen as unfit to govern, as incapable of rational decision making, but on the other hand society had entrusted to them one of the most important functions there is: the rearing of children. How, on the one hand, could women be considered incapable of making rational, political decisions, as morally unsuitable for the job of government and lead-ership, but on the other hand, capable of the rearing of children, which must include moral education? How could women – who were portrayed as weak, submissive, and in need of guardianship – at the same time be considered not only perfectly able to provide children (both boys and girls) with the necessary guidance, but uniquely and naturally designed for this role?

As a consequence of the fact that women's activities – despite the contradiction that Wollstonecraft pointed out – were deemed inferior to men, feminists argued that women were just as capable as men, and that nothing in their nature prohibited them from being just as good as men, given the opportunity. What needed to change in order for women to be given this opportunity? Women had to be granted the same political, economic, and legal rights as men. They had to be given the opportunity to be educated. There was, feminists argued, nothing inherent in women's abilities that precluded them from being just as good as men. They could be lawyers or doctors, or politicians. All they needed was to be given the chance, to be recognized as worthy of devel-oping the qualities that men were granted without question. In order to argue their case effectively, feminists often had recourse to the idea that they wanted to be seen as the same as men. What separated them from men was not any natural incapacity, not any inherent deficiency in their reasoning ability, but merely habit, and social conditioning. In 1869 in his essay 'On the Subjection of Women' John Stuart Mill (1983) argued this point forcefully. He pointed out that until women were given the opportunity to prove themselves, nobody was in a posi-tion to judge them incapable of reasoning well, being good politicians, or making sound political decisions. Convention alone dictated that women stay at home, restricting their roles to motherhood.

While the language of sex and gender was not developed until the 1960s, one could map the distinction between sex and gender onto some of the developments that preceded it. Beauvoir's famous proclamation that one is not born but becomes a woman could be read as challenging traditional patriarchal beliefs by differentiating between the two spheres that would later be labeled sex and gender. Traditionally, sex was posited as necessarily causing or determining gender. The relation between sex and gender has been construed as necessary by the tradition of patriarchy. To say that sex and gender are necessarily related to one another is to say that one causes or determines the other. Nature or sex is causally determinative of gender. The basic idea here is that 'Anatomy is Destiny.'

In contrast to the traditional model, which attributed feminine qualities to female sexuality, and masculine qualities to the male sex, feminists emphasized gender at the expense of sex, arguing, for example, that the relation between sex and gender is not necessary but arbitrary. Butler (1993) uses this formulation sometimes. Feminists thereby deflected attention away from the bodily or reproductive organs of the female body, and towards the idea that femininity is something that we are taught, something that is constructed or learned. If gender is a matter of socialization, the implication is that the emergence of new social norms will construct gender differently. If gender is something that is acquired through socialization or acculturation, it is also therefore something that can be unlearned, or reshaped. If emphasizing gender over sex accounted for the variability of gender over time and between cultures, it also appeared to facilitate change. Taken to its extreme, this view suggests either that there is no causal link between sex and gender, or that the causal determination is reversed – everything comes down to gender. It is not that there is a sexual foundation on the basis of which the normative dimensions of gender are created. Rather, due to cultural investments in the ideals of femininity and masculinity, the body is read according to preconceived ideas about gender, to the point that when physical anatomy does not accord with received ideas about sexual dimorphism, surgical intervention brings it into line with received ideas.

When the suffragettes chained themselves to railings in an attempt to have their political rights recognized, they argued that women had been unfairly excluded from the public realm and confined to the private domestic realm. Women had been confined to the role of mother and housewife, and considered unsuitable for the rigors and demands of the public realm – the realm of political debate, the realm of government. At bottom, what was required in order that women migrate out of the private and into the public realm was a redrawing of the boundary separating the private from the public. The demand to re-conceptualize this dividing line has become a mainstay of feminism. It was reflected in the 1960s slogan 'The personal is the political,' which encapsulated, for example, feminist challenges to violence against women in the home, and expressed women's demand to retain control of their bodies and freedom of choice with regard to abortion. hooks warns against reducing the idea that the personal is the political to an expression of some private experience of oppression, in which feminism degenerates into a personal plaint. Intent on highlighting the importance of emphasizing the political and social dimension of the feminist movement, hooks resists the idea that the experience of oppression amounts to an understanding of it, or is equivalent to a critical, political analysis of it. hooks' point can be restated in terms of a wariness about naïve versions of 'identity politics.' To take seriously the ideological construction of subjects is to be alert to the problems inherent in speaking from a particular position without problematizing that position as overdetermined by the forces it seeks to oppose. Subjects internalize oppressive ideologies, thereby reproducing pernicious myths that structure their self-understanding. Marx analyzed such a phenomenon under the heading of false-consciousness.

THE INVISIBLE WHITENESS OF MAINSTREAM FEMINIST THEORY: THE PUBLIC/PRIVATE DISTINCTION AS A CASE IN POINT

As we have learned from Foucault, power does not merely operate from the top down, it is not the unidirectional, monolithic force that classical Marxism took it to be. If power is everywhere, as Foucault argued, so too is resistance possible from multiple sources. Ideology is not all pervasive or determining. Women are not simply the dupes of men, just as racial minorities are not merely the victims or racism. hooks challenges the tendency of white feminist theorists to relegate African-American women to the sidelines, allowing them to voice their personal experience, permitting them to provide the racial perspective, parading them out in order to include 'authentic' examples of racial oppression in their analyses, without however conceding any fundamental challenge to the basic theoretical framework of white feminist ideology. At the same time, by making an intervention into feminist theory, hooks demands that white feminist theorists cede their unmarked authority over feminist discourse, requiring them to redefine their relationship to privilege, and begin to learn from, take seriously, and listen to the voices they have typically marginalized, albeit sometimes inadvertently. As Hazel Carby (2000) puts it: white women listen! Rather than defensively seeking to reassert their power over the terms of the discourse by finding new ways to marginalize the concerns of race theorists, occupying the position of white guilt or *ressentiment*, white women need to think through their implication in racism. This demands the rethinking of categories and distinctions that have been formative of feminist theory, shaping the contours of the debate. The history of feminist theory and praxis must be made accountable for its exclusivity.

Once it is established that mainstream feminism must confront its own racial, class, and heterosexist biases, not just by agreeing to be more inclusive while still maintaining control of what counts as feminist discourse, it becomes clear that its central categories, distinctions, and practices must remain available to constant scrutiny and re-examination. Feminism refuses to undertake such self-critical analysis so long as concepts such as race continue to function in a way that preserves the neutrality of whiteness, restricting the applicability of the term race to racial minorities, so that whenever we stipulate race, we continue to assume a model that preserves whiteness as the normative center, and specifies non-whites in relation to that center. To de-center an apparently race-neutral concept of gender is to overcome the tendency to envisage racially marked others as only relative to the dominant norm, comprehensible only in its terms.

Even when part of supposedly progressive feminist agendas, gender is racialized in ways that remain invisible to feminist theory. Presented as if it were neutral with regard to race and class, operating under the sign of equality, gender was refigured as an imperative capable of accomplishing the transition of women out of the private and into the public realm. Such refiguring failed to question, reconfigure, or thematize the racialization of the private space out of which women were seen as migrating, or the public space we were seen as accessing. That there is an implicit racialization on which the gendering of the private and public spaces rested, and which feminist praxis and theory neglected to thematize, can be made particularly clear in the case of the United States. One only has to think about the sense in which the public/private distinction that has been so formative in feminist mobilizations of the concept of gender, and was taken up as central to feminist theory, completely disregarded the role of immigrant or African-American domestic workers in the home. By stressing the need for women to move out of the private, domestic realm of the home, and into the public, political, masculine marked realm, feminism implicitly raced itself as white, as well as casting itself as middle class, and heterosexist. It failed to think about those women who worked in what was designated the private realm, whose work was carried out not in their own homes, but in the homes of more privileged women. Domestic labor was thereby raced and classed in ways that remain invisible and unthinkable for feminist theory, so long as it figures itself as the movement of women out of the private and into the public realm, as if this private space was not already politicized by racial and class divisions. By marking the private realm as feminine and the public realm as masculine, feminism continues to reproduce Hegelian political categories even as it challenges them, tacitly drawing a picture of its ideal woman as white, middle class, and heterosexual. It thereby ignores the large numbers of women who do not fit this stereotype. As Hazel Carby says, 'Ideologies of black female domesticity and motherhood have been constructed through their employment (or chattel position) as domestics and surrogate mothers to white families rather than in relation to their own families' (2000, 391). This renders their relationship to domesticity much more complicated and multi-layered than the simple equation between femininity and the private realm of the home that feminist theory set up in order to contest.

By pointing out that labor in the public sphere was remunerated, whereas labor in the home was unpaid, feminist Marxists repeated the error of rendering invisible those women who worked in the homes of others. The very terms in which the women's movement set itself up in the west thus relied on oppositions that rhetorically and structurally excluded women of color (see Mohanty 1991, 67). Needless to say, the legacy of slavery in the United States historically predetermined which women tended to work as domestic help, and which women tended to occupy the privileged classes able to hire them. If the slogan 'the personal is the political' has been a significant one for feminist theory, it must also be admitted that it has functioned in ways that replicate, condone, and reinvent racism. Unless you are white you don't really count as a person, in which case what is personal to you doesn't qualify as political to an invisibly white feminism.

Mainstream feminist articulation of the distinction between the private and the public realms has been a powerful way of making the argument for women's liberation, but part of its power resides in its unacknowledged yet structurally in-built racism. The organizing categories and slogans of feminism (public/private, the personal is the political) constructed the group 'women' in a way that remained oblivious to its invisible, normative, and raced dimensions. Feminism's blindness to its own rendering invisible of the concerns of some of the women it claimed to speak for calls for a re-mapping of its conceptual elaboration (see Bhattacharjee 1997). It requires a rethinking of the powerful symbolic role that the private/public distinction played within feminist discourse, as itself part of an exclusionary discourse that privileges the concerns of white, materially privileged women, without marking that privilege, or acknowledging its history. It demands that the constitutive role that race, class, and sexuality have played, precisely as exempted from gender, be acknowledged.

If the boundary between the private and the public has been a dominant theme for mainstream feminism, feminist conceptualizations of it have tended to reproduce the invisible whiteness of these categories. Mainstream feminism has construed the private, domestic, familial realm of the home in what amounts to western, hegemonic terms. Conceived as a patriarchal, heterosexual space, the private realm has figured as confining and restrictive, a space out of which women must migrate in order to liberate themselves, and realize the freedoms that men assume in the public space. This public space has been figured then as a space of freedom and liberation, characterized by the opportunity for work and education, and the protection of the law. The private is therefore marked as feminine, and the public as masculine, in an opposition that also inscribes racial presuppositions that have typically gone unmarked. Thus the very existence of domestic female workers, who might be undocumented immigrants, confounds any rigid opposition between the private and the public understood in mutual opposition to one another. Such women work in the homes of those who are more privileged, caring for the children and houses of privileged, middle-class women who can avail themselves of the opportunity to work in the masculine-identified, public realm while less privileged women care for their children. These domestic workers tend to occupy the lower classes, to be members of racial minorities, or to be immigrant workers, often undocumented. In the case of the latter group, not only do such domestic workers complicate any easy distinction of the private and the public realm, since they work in the homes of others, in which they also often live; immigrant workers also challenge the one-dimensional conception of the home as the domestic, familial space.

Bhattacharjee examines the multi-dimensional aspects of the notion of home, as it operates for South-Asian immigrant workers, for whom this notion extends beyond its traditional connotations of the patriarchal familial home. It also connotes the extended ethnic immigrant community on the one hand, and the country of origin on the other. If the concept of home itself contains multiple significations for immigrant women, similarly, the public realm cannot be understood purely as a realm that promises liberation and protection by the law. Since their legal status is often temporary, female domestic immigrant workers are often dependent on their husbands as sponsors to help them secure permanent legal residential rights. In order to prove that their marriages are not merely marriages of convenience, embarked upon merely for the sake of gaining legal immigrant status, such women must endure invasive state procedures, monitoring the 'validity' of their marriages. Such procedures manifest the coercive aspects of the state, which thereby represents not so much a potential liberatory space as a repressive force in the case of immigrants petitioning to gain permanent legal status. Far from protecting the rights of individuals, or providing a sanctuary to which women can appeal in order to obtain equal treatment, in this case the law invades the private space of the home in a way that differentiates between racially marked women and those who can assume their positions more readily in an allegedly unmarked public space.

Like immigrants who are victims of domestic violence, to whom Bhattacharjee compares immigrant domestic workers in this respect, undocumented immigrants demand that mainstream feminists reformulate both theories and practices that rely on a simplistic, racially blind dichotomy between public and private. Policies adopted by battered-women shelters have not typically been formulated in ways that foreground considerations of immigration and nationality. Insofar as such policies assume a racially homogeneous population, they will remain blind to the specific needs of racial minorities. Consequently, these policies will fail to reflect the needs and concerns of immigrant populations, who might be more than usually isolated due to language barriers and lack of familiarity with amenities in their adoptive countries. If shelters fail to address such concerns, the services they provide for victims of domestic violence will be geared only towards a select group of women.

The structuring assumptions of mainstream feminist theorizing around the demand for women's access to the public realm operate, then, on the basis of an uncomplicated, mutually exclusive, and racially unmarked opposition between the private and the public. To the extent that such rigid and dichotomous views reflect racial and class privilege, and help to inform policies that impact the resources available to racial minorities, the problem is not merely theoretical, but affects the safety of such women. Such assumptions are mirrored in characterizations of feminism as a struggle for civil rights that fail to address how the issues of civil rights and sovereignty play themselves out for various racial minorities. Achieving the vote might appear to be an uncontested good for all citizens. Reflection on the experience of native American women, on whom citizenship was forced by the 1924 *Indian Citizenship Act*, reveals that the matter is a good deal more complex. As Marie Anna Jaimes Guerrero (1997) argues, the cultural traditions and sovereignty of native American tribes, including matrilineal traditions, were erased by the imposition of a model of government based upon a partial replication of the US government. A judicial court system replaced tribal sovereignty, without being supplemented by the checks and balances provided by the separation of powers between the judiciary, legislative, and executive branches of government. The colonization of native American lands and ways of life replaced communal responsibility with an individualist, capitalist ethic, based on a Eurocentric social contract theory, whereby rights are conceptual-ized as conferred by government. These rights are envisaged, for example, by John Locke (1924), as inalienable – at least for those rec-ognized as fully human (slaves were not typically considered so by social contract theorists). Eliminating the collective character of tribal life, where difficulties were resolved through an informal network of duties and responsibilities, the state erected in its place an essentially corporate model of US government. Native American women became the ground upon which the tension between this colonial-style form of government and traditional tribal sovereignty was played out. Guerrero gives the example of Ms Martinez, a member of the Pueblo tribe who married a member of the Navajo tribe, and whose tribal membership, along with that of her children, was jeopardized. The newly instituted courts instituted by the *The Indian Reorganization Act* in 1934 and influenced by patriarchal, western traditions, excluded her from the Pueblo tribe. Ms Martinez was also excluded from membership of her husband's tribe, since the Navajo tribe operated according to matrilineal traditions.

RACE, CLASS, SEXUALITY, GENDER . . . AND MESSY HISTORIES: SUPPLEMENTING INTERSECTIONAL MODELS WITH DIACHRONIC ANALYSES

In an effort to correct the oversimplified feminist construction of gender as white, middle class, and heterosexual, a recent appeal to the intersections between gender, race, class, and sexuality has achieved prevalence. To ensure that the interlocking model of race, gender, and class is adequate to the complex, compacted, and historical configuration of how race is always already classed and gendered, or how gender is always already raced and classed, we need to undertake an analysis that does not remain blind to the intricate formation of each category. We need to avoid gesturing too easily and too readily towards some imagined, holistic community in which all our differences can, at least in theory, co-exist side by side with minimal tension. Even the notion of 'hybridity' does not adequately address the complexity of the issues that need to be addressed, since it still posits race, gender, and class as separable strands. To construe race, gender, and class as 'interlocking' (or overlapping, or intersecting, or hybrid) categories, terms, factors, or vectors, is to avoid treating these terms as if they had integrity in and of themselves, as if they could merely be added together. In fact, these 'categories' are always already indelibly shaped by one another, and their emergence at specific points in history is tied to a convoluted interdependence, in which they take on a particular historical configuration specific to a histor- ical epoch. Race, as a modern concept, emerges at a particular time (industrial, capitalist, colonialist). As such, its legibility inheres in dis- courses that have been constructed around the production of surplus value and organized not only around class tensions and competing myths of nationalism and colonialism, but also around ideologies of gender and sexuality. Gender, as a category mobilized by western feminists, takes shape initially as a white, middle class, heterosexist concept, but its emergence as a political category intended to specify all women renders invisible its race, class, and heterosexist biases.

The stipulation of race, class, and gender as 'interlocking' must avoid assuming the inviolability of these categories, and their analytic separability. If feminist theory is still in the process of redressing its racist history, race theory is still in the process of redressing its sexist history. To take another example of the complex and mutually constitutive nature of race and gender, third-world feminists have been criticized by postcolonial nationalists, who tend to occupy masculinist positions that go unmarked as such, for being corrupted by what is perceived as 'western' feminism. Such masculinist critiques of feminism implicitly construe feminism as white and western, tacitly consenting to the imperialist ownership of feminism. Postcolonial nationalists who chastise third-world feminists for selling out to feminism – as if feminism were owned by western women – are themselves acquiescing to the dictatorship of the colonizing powers they seek to put in question, by granting the white, western ownership of feminism. Postcolonial nationalism is thereby cast in the mold it purports to reject in its very attempt to defend some imaginary realm that is constituted as pure and uncorrupted by those values it posits as western. As Uma Narayan (1997) has shown, such defenses set in motion competing myths of nationalism that are highly selective, and which tend to pit the 'purity' and 'spirituality' of 'traditional' cultures against the alleged materialism and amorality of westerners. Since postcolonial nationalist myths are themselves called into being by the oppression and exploitation of the west, and since they are not only selective but also reactive, they are especially problematic representations of nationalism. Figured as guardians of the family and domesticity, as protectors of highly selective nationalist myths, women often become the ground upon which male postcolonial nationalists attempt to safeguard a version of 'their' culture – a culture which is in fact a construction that emerges in the first place only in reaction to colonization and in response to a mythical configuration of westernization. In the postcolonial quest to contest the forces of western imperialism, women are thus mobilized to safeguard nationalist myths of traditional cultures, as if these cultures could be purified of outside influences, as if they were not always already constructed in part in response to the history of colonialism – in short, as if these myths enjoyed some originary status. Women are thus constrained by atavistic roles as the defenders of 'traditional' culture, the features of which are determined in opposition to a mythical version of westernization that is just as selective as the post-colonial nationalist myth against which it is pitted. Clearly, in order to make sense of how race and nationalism are figured within post-colonial discourse one has also to analyze gender, which turns out to have played a significant constitutive role in the construction of the specific racial and nationalist configurations that have played themselves out between east and west.

POSTCOLONIAL FEMINIST THEORY MEETS PHENOMENOLOGY

Postcolonial feminist theory requires race theory to be responsible for its gender biases as much as it requires philosophy to be accountable for its racial and gender universalism. As such it does not rest content with the parameters established by the philosopher and social critic widely regarded as the founder of postcolonial studies, although it unquestionably builds on the edifice he established. Frantz Fanon's phenomenological account of the alienation produced under the white colonial gaze both draws on the ontologies of Jean-Paul Sartre and Maurice Merleau-Ponty and challenges those ostensibly universal ontologies to be accountable for their exclusions. 'Jean-Paul Sartre had forgotten,' Fanon tells us, 'that the Negro suffers in his body quite differently from the white man' (1967, 138). Fanon's oft cited phenomenological account of the disintegration he experiences when he sees himself through the eyes of the white other, whose gaze is structured by the distorting and dehumanizing myths of cannibalism, animality, and primitivism, establishes the asymmetry of the gaze. The transformation of the bodily schema is brought about through these alienating myths and legends that constitute what Fanon calls the 'historico-racial schema' (Fanon 1967, 111). As Jeremy Weate says, the gaze of the other is structured by a 'white imaginary' (Weate 2001, 174), which is informed by the 'myth of the negro' (Fanon 1967, 117; 114). Once this mythic imaginary establishes a hold on Fanon's relationship to the world, there is a 'slippage' (Weate 2001, 173–4) or reduction of the historico-racial schema, fabricated by the myth of the negro, to the 'racial epidermal schema' (Fanon 1967, 112). The white masks of stupidity, bestiality, and inferiority are stripped away to reveal what now appears to ground them: a black skin. Thus Fanon reveals the process by which black skin has come to signify primitivism and bestiality, and in the process he provides, as Weate puts it, a 'genealogy' of racial essentialism.

The failure of ontology to take account of the way in which the racialized, embodied relationship of subjects to the world is constructed through the intervention of a white gaze signifies the need to recast phenomenology. The past catches up with the present, imprisoning Fanon in a web of meanings that reduce him to an object, and inhibiting his freedom, creativity, and transcendence. Paralyzed by his reflection in the eyes of the white other, he is demeaned, unable to act, and disabled in his attempts to make a meaningful intervention in the world that could transform history.

If Fanon's work exhibits the pervasive influence of phenomenology and existentialism, the influence of psychoanalysis is also decisive. Psychoanalytic theory has remained surprisingly productive for race theorists, who continue to draw inspiration from it, despite their legitimate claims that its theoretical inclination is permeated with western presuppositions. Fanon, who observes with Malinowski the compulsion of western ethnologists to find 'the complexes of their own civilization . . . duplicated in the people they study' (Fanon 1967, 152; 143), remains exemplary in this respect. It is clear that Fanon is by no means completely persuaded by psychoanalytic theory, and remains skeptical about the applicability of the Oedipus complex to the people of the French Antilles (see 152; 143), even refusing the idea that white racism is unconscious (see Fanon 1968). Yet it is also clear that the concepts of the unconscious, trauma, catharsis, projection, phobia, and fetishism infuse his powerful evocation of the bodily fragmentation he undergoes, a suffering that he describes with reference to the disintegration of the corporeal or bodily schema. Fanon emphasizes that the reduction of blacks to a racial epidermal schema is facilitated in part by the equation of blacks with sexuality. This eroticization takes the shape of myths that Fanon gives voice to when he says, 'As for Negroes, they have tremendous sexual powers. What do you expect, with all the freedom they have in their jungles! They copulate at all times and in all places. They are really genital. They have so many children that they cannot even count them. Be careful, or they will flood us with little mulattoes' (Fanon 1967, 157; 148). The concern with miscegenation that Fanon registers here is one that runs throughout his reflections, and it is precisely here that his disturbing tendency to reproduce uncritically some of the most denigrating attitudes about female sexuality manifests itself. Fanon's reproduction of such myths is, of course, in the name of his parodic representation of white patriarchy. Whiteness and patriarchy, however, are not homologous with one another. As Fanon attempts to draw out the complicity of white women with the 'myth of the negro,' there are moments at which his account of women falls prey to a mythology of women that needs to be brought into question just as rigorously as Fanon brings into question the 'myth of the negro.' When he says, 'Our women are at the mercy of the Negroes' (Fanon 1967, 157; 143) he is clearly speaking in the voice of white patriarchy, and at certain points he acknowledges that white women are rendered pathological in a way that parallels black experience (see 1967, 159; 149). Yet it is not enough to establish such parallels without exploring how race usurps gender stereotypes and gender usurps racist stereotypes. It is disappointing that, despite his astute analysis of racial mythology, Fanon is unable to bring to bear his analytical skills with equal facility in order to expose how sexual mythology denigrates women. He continues to reduce women to the property of men, to construe women as the passive repositories of male desire, and to project onto women violent fantasies that perhaps enact a displacement of his own suffering. So we find Fanon reproducing such mythology without taking any critical distance from it: 'Since we have learned to know all the tricks the ego uses in order to defend itself, we know too that its denials must in no case be taken literally. Are we not now observing a complete inversion? Basically, does this *fear* of rape not itself cry out for rape? Just as there are faces that ask to be slapped, can one not speak of women who ask to be raped?' (Fanon 1967, 156; 147). The dangerous and pernicious myth that women are crying out for rape, or asking to be raped, has much more to do with a masculine imaginary that constructs a fantasy of women as available, peripheral, and dispensable, than it does with what women want. As Rey Chow argues, Fanon's assumption that women want to be raped, and as such are unrapable, 'ultimately minimizes if not effaces the racial and ethnic differences between black and white women' and 'portrays women's sexuality in the main as characterized by an active, sadomasochistic desire – to be raped, to rape herself, to rip herself open' (1999, 45). The masculine imaginary that he takes over uncritically from phenomenology and psychoanalysis prevents Fanon from seeing women in their full subjectivity. It intervenes in his construction of women so that while he dismantles the white masks that cover black skins with such precision, he continues to see women through a masculinist mask: as inconsistent, incapable of saying what we mean or of knowing what we want, as inviting violence.

Perhaps if Fanon had not restricted his thematization of the hypersexualization of blacks to men he might have been able to render problematic, instead of perpetuate, such sexist myths. Instead it is left to critics such as Lola Young to extend to women the purview of how blacks have been represented by the white imaginary. 'In the case of both females and males, the contention that blacks are oversexed is historically linked to and "proven" by alleged anatomical excesses in one form or another' (2000, 273). Evelynn Hammonds shows how 'black women's sexuality has been constructed in a binary opposition to that of white women: it is rendered simultaneously invisible, visible (exposed), hypervisible, and pathologized in dominant discourses' (1997, 170). On the one hand 'European commentators' ascribed ' "primitive" genitalia' to African black women which were then defined 'as the sign of their "primitive" sexual appetites' (172). This is consonant with the hypervisibility of black women's sexuality, which was constructed as 'inherently immoral and uncontrollable' (ibid.) and defined in opposition to white women's sexuality. 'White women were characterized as pure, passionless, and de-sexed, while black women were the epitome of immorality, pathology, impurity, and sex itself' (173). On the other hand, black women's sexuality has been consigned to the realm of the invisible, in part because, in reaction to the consistently hyperbolic representations of black female sexuality, black women resorted to a 'politics of silence' (175). This 'imposed production of silence' both deprived black women of the 'ability to articulate any conception of their sexuality' (177) and exacerbated the effacement or invisibility of black women achieved by the distortions of colonial representations. These representations relied upon an 'always already colonized black female body' such that the black female is constructed 'as the embodiment of sex' while black women are 'unvoiced, unseen – everything that is not white' (171).

The fact that a politics of silence was produced in response to the excessive visibility to which black female sexuality has been subject by a white, patriarchal, colonialist imaginary might go some way toward explaining how critics such as Fanon can recycle the dominant view. Just as Fanon found it necessary to draw attention to the universalism of Sartre and Merleau-Ponty, Freud and Lacan, in order to show that the asymmetrical racial positions that existed in the world were covered over by their phenomenological and psychoanalytic attempts to generalize human experience, so women who read Fanon are faced with the question of how to respond to his failure to fully think through the sexism in which his own postcolonial philosophy remains implicated.

Not only must feminist theory confront its own history of race-blindness, but race theory must also confront its gender-blindness. Since the race partiality of feminist theory and the gender partiality of race theory are embedded in the development of their formal apparatus, to address these biases is a difficult theoretical undertaking. Gender is already raced, and race is already gendered, although the ways in which gender is racially inflected and race is inflected by gender have gone unthematized. The comparative logic of the political identities implicit in the additive model of race, gender, and class is evident not only in some feminist thinking but also in attempts to apply the experience of one racial minority to another, as if the content of minority experiences mirrored one another. We need to be self-critical even of that work, by asking whether it really manages to get at the phenomena it aims for.

The fluidity of life, together with the rigidity of categories, bequeaths us – those of us who are interested in philosophical clarity and political transformation in the name of justice – a complex series of problems. This nexus of problems can be illuminated under the heading of fetishism. Marx has analyzed the problem of commodity fetishism in great detail and with great acumen, albeit in a way that leaves unaddressed a number of other problems, even as his method of historical materialism continues to provide resources for the formulation of these problems. Foucault has developed this in the direction of a micro-politics, in which power is operative in multiple and contested sites, and where the historical specificity of discourses of sexuality disposes of shifting categories such that sexual deviance, once the province of the priest in the confessional box, becomes subject to the authority of medical experts, whose knowledge helps to produce sexually deviant subjects not as sinful, but as pathologized. The locus of authority having shifted from the church to the psychoanalyst's couch, those responsible for the production of knowledge and the constitution of sexualities occupy different positions in the nexus of power relations within which subjects strive to signify themselves as legitimate, both to themselves and others.

Their respective models of power, both indebted to and departing from classical Marxism, have in turn informed divergent feminist models of thought. At the same time, a constellation of feminist theorists have introduced new, and sometimes mutually incompatible, analyses, which build on, challenge, and take further insights introduced by Marx and Engels, and re-evaluated in a wholesale way by Foucault. Heidi Hartmann will serve as our starting point for examining these issues.

CHAPTER 2

FEMINISM AND MARXISM: THE USEFULNESS AND THE LIMITATIONS OF PARALLEL MODELS

As Marx understood in his analysis of alienation, and of the estrangement of commodity fetishism, social relations appear to be governed by static, implacable forces. Relations between humans take on the appearance of relations between things – they become reified. Capital appears to govern the relations between humans, which take on the appearance of fixity and necessity. Only once a new form of production emerges, which provides an alternative to the commodity form, can the authority of commodities be challenged. The genius of capitalism lies in its ability to reproduce itself not merely at the material level, but also at the ideological level. If Louis Althusser has analyzed the forms in which ideology reproduces itself at the institutional level, in the shape of religion, education, and the family, Antonio Gramsci has emphasized the extent to which what appears to be the common sense of received ideas (e.g. the idea that feminism must be about equality) in fact derives from the dominant ideology of those in power. Our consent to such ideas is manufactured by the prevailing interests of the ruling class – to adapt Noam Chomsky's formulation – or, for instance, those who occupy elite positions in relation to feminist theory. Typically, white, privileged women have defined the terms of the feminist debate, and consequently have been able to overlook forms of social inequality dictated by class oppression or racial discrimination. This hegemonic relation to what is admitted as feminist, and what is rejected, perpetuates the marginalization of those who have traditionally occupied less privileged roles.

Set in Nova Scotia, the film *Margaret's Museum* focuses on the stories of the working-class women who are left behind when their husbands, sons, and brothers become casualties of the coal mining monopoly that dominates the rural Canadian community. Death is a routine part of working in the mine, which prioritizes profits over safety. As the working conditions of the mine systematically neglect the safety of its workers, capitalism erodes the Gaelic culture of its inhabitants, leveling their activity to that consonant with the production of profit. Signaling yet another accident in the mine, the siren goes off, and Margaret (Helena Bonham Carter), finds herself widowed at an early age, having also lost her grandfather, father, and two brothers to the mine. The film explores not only the economic toll that these deaths take, but their psychic toll. Unable to tolerate the way in which the mine exploits the community, callously treating its workers by showing no respect for their lives, Margaret's response is that of someone who has borne as much as she can. Refusing the intolerable burden of suffering and dehumanization that the mine foists upon her, and recoiling from the usual conventions of mourning which would sanitize the horrific neglect of safety standards by the mining company, she reacts in a way that draws attention to the impact of those working conditions on the bodily organs of the miners. She opens a museum where she puts on display the lungs of her grandfather, and those of her husband in order to show the difference between black lung – the disease that caused her grandfather's death – and healthy lungs. Having only recently and reluctantly conceded to work in the mine so that he and Margaret can afford to have children, her husband Neil has healthy lungs. Margaret's museum is her way of protesting the dehumanization of the mining monopoly, which calculates the death of its workers as just one of those unavoidable aspects of its unremitting goal: to extract as much surplus value as possible, no matter what the cost in human life. Margaret intends to show an unwitting public what healthy lungs look like, compared to the lungs of her grandfather. For her trouble, she is arrested and incarcerated in an asylum. Her attempt to display the irrationality and immorality of a capitalist system that calculates death as part of the price of coal is itself punished as irrational, as insane – a punishment, then, that recuperates as rational and sane the deadly calculations of the mining company, blind to the value of human life, with eyes only for profit. A punishment, too, that resonates with a long history in which women have been trivialized and manipulated through their association with madness.

Heidi Hartmann has aptly characterized the relationship between feminism and Marxism as an 'unhappy marriage,' one in which

Marxism has proved itself dominant. Marxist feminists must either work towards a better relationship, suggested Hartmann, or get a divorce. Hartmann argues for a healthier alliance between feminism and Marxism, pointing out that Marxist categories of analysis are blind to the dynamics of gender. Reducing gender to class, Marxism ends up subsuming feminism: Marxism and feminism are one, and that one is Marxism. Geared to the categories of labor and production, and based on a patriarchal model of the worker, Marxist theory could only be applied to women either by lumping them in with the apparently generic category of laborer – a category that in fact refers to a masculinized model – or by reinforcing the gendered expectation that women's work was in the home, and that Marxist categories were inapplicable to it.

Although women have long been part of the workforce, patriarchal ideology has failed to acknowledge the central role that women have played in the relations of production. The tendency has been to construe women as having a privileged relation to reproduction and to exclude them from an analysis of production. No doubt assumptions about a natural division of labor, based on reproductive differences, underlie such a tendency.

A third way of applying Marxist categories to women is to parse out women's role in the reproduction of the workforce, both at the level of day-to-day rejuvenation and at the level of generational reproduction. Women facilitate the reproduction of capitalist processes in the form of housework, which replenishes the worker, enabling him to return to work day in and day out, with a full stomach and clean clothes, with enough energy to sustain him as a productive laborer. Women also ensure, through procreation, the continuous availability of the workforce. The result is that women's roles can only be accounted for by an economic, class analysis, an analysis that remains blind, for example, to the hidden dimension that women's unpaid work in the home, in the form of housework, adds to the value of commodities. The problem with construing housework as the ultimate form of surplus value is that it conforms to the original problematic that Hartmann tried to avoid, namely the subsumption of feminism by Marxist theory.

Marxist theory appeals to a projected future in which working-class interests are realized as universal, yet the historical record shows that far from being universal, even the interests of the working class are divided by both gender and race. In its apparently infinite versatility, capitalism functions in a way that adapts both to patriarchy and to racism. Exemplary of its flexibility was the introduction and prevalence of the 'family wage,' a wage that acknowledged the status of men as head of the household. Working-class men and capitalist men found a common cause in arguing for differential wages for men and women. Patriarchy divided the interests of the working class by perpetuating the idea that men should be paid a higher wage than women, and capitalism adapted accordingly. The wage differential discouraged women from joining the workforce, providing them with an incentive to remain in the house and perform the household tasks that traditionally would have been considered proper to women: cooking, shopping, cleaning, and rearing children.

With the rise in multinational corporations, in the wake of increased competition among advanced, western, capitalist economies, the global, transnational character of capitalism underscores the need for feminist theory not only to supplement Marxism's focus on class economics with an analysis of gender, but also to extend its consideration to race and ethnicity. As manufacturing industries continue to relocate to developing countries, where overhead costs are relatively low, unemployment rates are often high, and worker organization is often barely existent, exploitation of third world women is particularly acute. Especially attractive to labor-intensive manufacturing industries, such as clothing and electronics, outsourcing ensures a supply of low-cost goods for western societies, only by maintaining low wage levels for workers in third world countries. In relative terms, third world women are paid the lowest wages – lower than men in both developing and developed countries, and lower than women in developed economies. The continuing growth of capitalism in developing countries ensures neither that their women workers will benefit from higher wages, nor that their relative exploitation will decline. Even when women are promoted, it is usually to occupy positions that have been vacated by men, who themselves have moved on to more powerful or lucrative positions, so that patriarchal forces ensure women's continued relative exploitation.

As international trade has augmented, competition has increased between advanced capitalist countries such as Japan, the Western European countries, and the United States, fuelling the motivation to reduce costs of production. As capitalism developed in other countries, such as Singapore and Hong Kong, the developed nations found themselves competing not only with one another, but also with developing countries, who engaged in multinational offshore operations in other developing countries. In order to compete successfully with their relatively low costs of production, capitalist owners of the means of production in the developed world relocated their manufacturing plants to these same countries, creating an international division of labor. Such relocation is often encouraged by the governments of developing countries in the form of tax breaks, subsidies, and attractive financial packages.

Sweatshop conditions are not limited to developing countries; immigrant workers can be subject to poor working conditions and below minimum wages in the developed world too. Homeworkers, such as third world women electronics workers in the Silicon Valley or black women workers in small, family run businesses in Britain, are also open to abusive and exploitative practices, both at the material and ideological levels (Mohanty 1997). Such workers lack job protection, workers' rights or benefits at the same time as their work is seen merely as an extension of their familial duties. In the case of lacemakers in Nasarpur, India, who are designated by, and accept, the label 'housewives,' such work is not recognized as labor, but understood to be continuous with the other tasks that women typically perform in the household, including household chores and childcare. Their designation as 'housewives' symbolically identifies women workers as defined by heterosexual marriages, in relation to their husbands, thereby depriving them of identities as women workers, and erasing any platform they might otherwise have, on the basis of which to organize. Rendering them invisible as workers, and maintaining their isolation in discrete, conjugal homes effectively deprives them of any collective bargaining power. It also allows the women to reconcile the work they do with traditional, patriarchal ideas of womanhood, without challenging the ideology that defines women as homemakers.

Central to Marxist analyses is the theory of surplus value, although it was left to feminist theorists to reflect on how the theory of surplus value might apply to that work which is typically unremunerated and relegated to women, namely housework. Capitalism succeeds by increasing profits: the more profits accumulate, the more money becomes available for capital investment. The more factories are owned, the more workers can be employed; the more workers are employed, the more goods can be produced; the more goods are produced, and the cheaper the costs of production, the greater the profits for the capitalist owners of the means of production. Surplus value is the difference between what the capitalist owner of production pays the workers, usually determined by whatever it takes in order to ensure their biological survival, and the amount that commodities can command on the market. In other words, surplus value is the difference between, on the one hand, what it costs to keep the labor force alive – what it costs to pay workers subsistence wages – and the exchange value of the commodity on the other. Profits are made by increasing the gap between the cost of the means of subsistence, or how much the capitalist pays workers to maintain production, and the amount for which commodities are sold.

Whereas the use value of a product is determined by its function – the use value of a coat is to keep its wearer warm, or the use value of a loaf of bread is to satisfy hunger – the exchange value is the amount of money for which a particular commodity can be sold. By establishing a common denominator that can mediate between material goods, money provides us with a universal exchange system. It abstracts from the particular use value of an object, at the same time reducing the material differences between various goods to a common value, represented by money. Through this process of abstraction, the sensuous character of the commodity is negated. The grain or type of the wood that is used to make a table does not figure in the equation that determines how many chairs can be exchanged for the table, just as the skills of a carpenter are rendered invisible when they are leveled out in order to be measured according to some ratio that establishes one form of labor as equivalent units of another. The abstraction from the sensuous materiality of both the product and the process of labor to a universal value that facilitates the exchange of diverse goods cancels out particularity.

The exchange value of a designer t-shirt will not be the same as that of an ordinary t-shirt, even though their use values are identical. As consumers, we are willing to pay more for brand name clothes than we are for clothes which serve exactly the same function, namely keeping us warm. For the sake of fashion, we buy Levi jeans or Nike trainers. Consumption is driven not by need, but by desire: we are encouraged to believe that we just must have that new BMW, or that new dress, not because our old car or clothes have lost their use value, but because they are no longer in fashion – they do not make the same statement. As a society of consumers, we appear to be driven by our desire to have the latest model, a situation that Marxists describe in terms of commodity fetishism. Consumer-citizens are governed by things, which become our gods – the gods of the market-place. We worship commodities, and are driven continually to buy more, not because we necessarily need them, but because we want to keep up appearances, to compete with the neighbors, to be like every-one else. We fetishize material things, becoming slaves to commodi-ties. No longer in control of the goods produced by the capitalist system, we come to be controlled by them. In a strange reversal, material objects come to command our lives, as the commodification of society confers on the process of material acquisition an appar-ent necessity. The social or human relations that stand behind the commodities are obscured, as we come to be governed by the imper-sonal, inhuman laws of the marketplace, and not by our own voli-tion. The relations of human labor that in fact lie behind the production of commodities are only represented by the abstract value of money, a representation that reifies human relations, making them appear to be determined by market forces, as if the commodities themselves had natural powers over us.

Since Marxist analyses focused upon the categories of labor and production, and the public, masculinized realm of the workplace, they tended to neglect the role of housework, typically performed by women. In response, feminist theorists insisted that not only the process of production, but also the process of reproduction are central to the success of capitalist enterprises. The reproduction of the worker occurs not just at the biological level in the form of pro-creation, a process that ensures the constant availability of new workers, but also at the daily level of rejuvenation and replenishment of physical energy. When the worker returns home after a hard day's work, he needs food to eat, liquid to drink, a chair to rest in, and a bed to sleep in. Certain tasks must be performed in order to convert the goods that are brought home with his wages into a meal, or a comfortable place in which to rest. The food must be cleaned, pre-pared, and cooked before it is put on the table, ready to consume. Clothes must be washed, dried, and ironed before they can be worn to work the next day. The sheets must be laundered, and the bed must be made before it can provide a good night's rest. The labor per-formed in order to send the worker back to work refreshed the next day remains invisible to Marxism, precisely because that labor is unpaid. The reproduction of the worker is facilitated by housework, but not calculated into Marx's theory of surplus value. Marx focused on the difference between subsistence-level wages and exchange value in order to compute surplus value. It could be argued, however, that housework is the ultimate or supreme locus of surplus value. It goes completely unrecognized, and uncompensated, and yet it adds value to the commodities that are produced and sold. It is hardly surprising that the response of some feminists, such as Shulamith Firestone (1972), to such a situation was to argue that women should be paid for their housework.

The capitalist system reproduces itself at the material level by ensuring a continued supply of workers, and by relying on an unacknowledged source of labor in the form of housework. A second aspect of the way in which the capitalist system reproduces itself, and thereby ensures its continuation, is at the ideological level. Children are brought up to obey their parents, and at the same time they are trained to be obedient workers. Class and gender ideologies permeate this upbringing, conveying the idea that women's place is in the home, and men's role is to be the provider. The reproduction of patriarchal and capitalist ideology finds expression not only in the family, but also in religious organizations, schools, clubs, armies, and other institutions. The capitalist machinery keeps on turning, and with it, the idea that workers are dispensable is reproduced. The worker is essentially replaceable and dispensable: one worker can be substituted for another. Through the dehumanization, alienation, and self-estrangement of the worker, the worker is distanced from the product he makes (since he does not own it, and probably could not afford to do so), from his creative process (which is undertaken for the sake of the profit of capitalism, and not for his own ends), from his co-workers, and from himself. Organization of workers' rights in the form of unions, for example, is discouraged. Workers fear for their jobs, in the knowledge that someone else is ready and willing to step up and take their place. This results in their acquiescence to low wages and poor working conditions. Workers are thus kept in their place, especially in conditions of high unemployment, knowing that there is a reserve army of laborers waiting to step into their shoes. Such problems are particularly acute where government regulations ensuring worker protection are ineffective or non-existent, and where any attempt on behalf of the workers to organize or form unions is met with their immediate dismissal.

The harsh punishment that is often meted out to those workers who attempt to organize in order to protect and augment workers' rights has not succeeded, however, in dissuading workers' resistance. Examples of such resistance include women workers in Korea, who moved into a factory in Masan in order to stop production, cooked and ate their meals in the factory, guarded the machines, and effectively stopped production. The symbolic message of such resistance resonates with the difficulty of imposing any strict dividing line between the private realm of the home and the public domain of work. The strike of the Korean women demonstrates the impossibility of separating home from work, the private from the public, in any absolute manner.

With the development of global capitalism, and the increase of outsourcing, workers in advanced capitalist economies are fearful that their jobs will be exported to third world countries, where wages are lower, overhead costs are less, and working conditions are worse. While such fears are justified, and such threats have a disproportionate impact on the working class, it is equally true that the threshold of expectation in the west is significantly higher than in developing countries. The lifestyle of those living under advanced forms of capitalism has been significantly shaped first by colonization, and then by the 'recolonization' effected by global capitalism, whereby cheap goods are available in the west only at the cost of high levels of exploitation in the developing world. In their quest to increase profits, multinational corporations have shifted attention away from the division of labor analyzed by classical Marxism and towards an international division of labor. The division of labor no longer operates simply along gender lines, according to which the sphere of reproduction is the work of women, while the realm of production is considered a masculine domain. Increasingly, race, ethnicity, and caste become paramount in orchestrating the 'spatial economy' of the international labor force. Chandra Talpade Mohanty (1997) points out that companies target racialized minority groups by deskilling labor processes, thereby making production processes even more repetitive and tedious than they would otherwise be, and drawing on racist, nativist stereotypes to justify such targeting. Accordingly, Asian women are expected to acquiesce to the demands of unskilled labor – after all, the story goes, they are used to such work, coming from pre-agricultural, pre-modern societies.

Multinational companies try to justify their exploitation of workers in third world countries by claiming that due to lower costs of living, workers do not need high wages. Yet such rationales often conflict with the facts on the ground. The documentary *Mickey Mouse goes to Haiti* examines the working conditions in factories owned by Walt Disney in Haiti, making the point that it would be highly unusual for a worker to have 20 gourds at the end of the day with which to purchase food to feed her family, and that this amount would be grossly inadequate to do so. The wages are so low that workers live on credit, pawn their belongings, and often have no money to purchase food even on pay day.

Activists focusing on the sweatshop conditions in which multinational corporations maintain third world women workers point out that the solution is not to force such companies to withdraw or close down. Often, despite atrocious working conditions, such companies offer alternatives to workers that are better than those offered by local companies. Often too, some paid work is better than no paid work, albeit poorly paid. Activists therefore focus on demanding a living wage for third world workers, and on improving working conditions, rather than forcing companies to close down their operations, which could ultimately be more detrimental to workers with severely limited possibilities for any alternative income.

Just as it is important not to represent third world women workers merely as victims, but also to acknowledge their active resistance to capitalist, patriarchal, and racist exploitation, so it is important to avoid construing commodity fetishism as all pervasive and all determining. As consumers, we do not simply stand in a passive relationship to a manipulative marketplace, which succeeds in selling us dreams of beauty, happiness, and success. We are not simply duped by commodities, rather we develop creative relationships with commodities, integrating them into our lives in ways that do not necessarily enshrine them as having a god-like, magical power over us. We are capable of occupying our roles as consumers in ways that demystify commodity fetishism, by not allowing social relations to be obscured by relations between things, in ways that are critical, informed, and politically aware. We can educate ourselves about the companies we support. We can choose to buy products made by companies that maintain good working conditions for their workers. To be savvy consumers is not necessarily to boycott certain companies, but rather to find ways of pressuring them to improve conditions for their workers.

IS FEMINISM TO MARXISM AS LESBIAN THEORY IS TO FEMINIST THEORY?

Initially, the conceptual problematic Hartmann outlines operates as a useful lens through which to focus not only the uneasy yet productive relationship that has subsisted between feminism and Marxism, but also a new set of difficulties that arise in the parallelism that emerges in feminist attempts to render feminist theory inclusive. In order to analyze both the advances that various feminist thinkers have contributed in this context, and their drawbacks, it will be helpful to propose the tensions feminist theory is currently in the process of negotiating in terms of the following impasse. Starting from a dominant theory, such as Marxism, feminists have often proposed a model that seeks to use the insights of a given position by construing its positive aspects as amenable to feminist theory, while problematizing its negative aspects and demonstrating them to be blind to considerations of sex/gender. The aim is to establish the need for a more harmonious relationship between, in this case, Marxism and feminism, of the sort that is both sensitive to the blindspots of both, and capable of recuperating what is best in both. Hence, Hartmann takes up the Marxist method of historical materialism as a valuable tool, while criticizing Marxist theory for its sex-blind approach. Marxism reduces sex to class, subsuming feminism under Marxism, so that women can only figure in a way that acknowledges their membership of one of two groups: the oppressed working class, or the proletariat, on the one hand, and the owners of the means of production, the bourgeoisie, the middle class, or the capitalist oppressor on the other. This analysis leaves no room for acknowledging that within whichever group of workers women are included, patriarchy and capitalism work hand in hand to discriminate against women, who tend to occupy employment positions that are lower on the totem pole – service workers, health workers, etc. – and whose wages are systematically lower than those of their male counterparts.

Neither does this analysis leave any room for acknowledging the role that housework has traditionally played in the creation of surplus value. Since housework is unpaid, and the Marxist analysis depends upon construing surplus value as that which results from the difference between the exchange value of a product (determined by market forces) and the cost of raw materials, overhead costs, and the amount it takes to maintain and reproduce the worker (subsistence-level wages), it remains blind to the contribution housework makes to capitalist profits. As we have seen, some feminists have attempted to correct this scenario by inscribing housework into the story that Marxism tells about the extraction of surplus value. In an inspired move, that also turns out to be flawed from the perspective of Hartmann's argument, Della Costa (quoted by Hartmann) rewrites Marxist theory to take account of women's labor, while feminists such as Firestone (1972) take it one step further to argue that housework should be paid. Yet from Hartmann's perspective, the trouble with such moves is that they reiterate, albeit in a new way, the original relationship of subservience between feminism and Marxism. Once again, feminism becomes the handmaiden of Marxism, a mere vehicle for the expression of the higher truth of economic analysis, just one more example to confirm Marxism's global reach, rather than offering an insight that is incompatible, irreducible to, and finally irreconcilable with the Marxist framework. Insofar as Marxism remains blind to sex, insofar as it analyzes the mechanisms and social divisions of capitalism in terms that accept the fundamental class opposition between the owners of the means of production and the workers, it can only ever account for women insofar as they are workers – unpaid or not. It cannot account for women as discriminated against on the basis of our sex. It cannot explain why women in the workforce are not promoted at the rate that men are, why they are not considered to be managerially competent, why they are not paid the same wages or salaries as men even when the jobs they perform are of equal worth or identical to those of men. In a nutshell, writing housework into the analysis of surplus value, as brilliant a move as it might be, turns out, like many brilliant moves, to be profoundly flawed. According to the logic of Hartmann's analysis, and according to its prevailing image, what we need is not a repetition of the same logic, so that Marxist categories are extended to include women, but a better marriage between feminism and Marxism, so that Marxism does not subsume feminism. Either we need a healthier relationship, or we need a divorce. What we don't need is just one more attempt to claim that Marx (or Hegel, Freud, Heidegger, Lacan, Levinas, or Derrida for that matter) saw it all, and even if he didn't, his theory can be adapted to make it look as if he did.

The full irony – and heterosexism – of Hartmann's call for a better marriage between Marxism and feminism comes to the fore in

Cheshire Calhoun's (1994) self-conscious appropriation and reinvention of Hartmann's prevailing image. Taking up the guiding
image with which Hartmann provided us and applying its logic to
the relationship between feminism and lesbian theory, Calhoun's
meticulous mapping out of this logic demonstrates the conceptual
dilemma within which thinkers as crucial for feminist theory as
Judith Butler and Monique Wittig nonetheless find themselves
mired. Could it be that even Butler, for all her brilliance – finds
herself replicating the logic of patriarchy? According to Calhoun's
persuasive analysis the answer is a resounding yes. How, then, does
Calhoun issue this challenge, sweeping along with it many of the
insights that some diehard 'French feminists' had come to accept
without question? Let's start with Wittig, whose influence on
Butler's early formulations is well-established (see 1990).

Wittig makes a potent and controversial claim, namely that lesbians exit the category of woman. In order to understand its force,
let's briefly recall the analyses of thinkers of the ilk of Christine
Delphy (1993) and Colette Guillamin (1999). In itself something of
a tour de force, Delphy's work maps out for us in clear and cogent
terms the trajectory of feminist theory, beginning with anthropolo-
gist Margaret Mead. Essentially, Delphy accomplishes an inversion.
According to patriarchal tradition – and according to many versions
of feminist thought – sex precedes gender. That is, biology, anatomy,
physiology, nature, DNA structure, genetics, materiality, 'the body' –
or however one expresses it – comes before, logically and chronologically (as Julia Kristeva is so fond of saying – though not in this
context), social structures, gendered roles, historically engendered
expectations and preconceptions, cultural mores, prescriptions and
taboos on sexual behavior, and so on. Delphy puts us through our
paces and ends up claiming that the reverse is true. It is not that
bodies, nature, or materiality precede social structures, culture, or
history. Rather, it is the other way around: gender precedes sex. The
logic goes like this. We posit some ostensibly natural ground from an
always already cultural point of view, and then we start to act like it
was always there, as if it were some necessary, unchanging, Platonic
essence or ideal, pre-existing us, eternal in its verity. Such a positing
serves a variety of purposes. It reassures us, makes us feel like we
are on firm ground, the *terra firma* holding us up and justifying us
in our quirky, historically produced, cultural beliefs about who we
are, who we should be, and what possibilities should bind us. To read

a heterosexist paradigm on to the body is to construe sex as merely procreative, reproduction of the species as the be all and end all of humanity; it is to act as if sexual dimorphism were natural instead of normative, to assume that there are two and only two sexes, whose mutually exclusive 'nature' were writ large. It is to forget that hermaphrodites have existed since time immemorial, to sidestep the issue of intersexuality, to forget that surgical intervention has systematically attempted to erase anatomical ambiguity by imposing the socially inculcated ideals of female and male anatomy on infants before they are capable of consent, before they can tell us who or what they think they are. All this in the name of gender conformity, all in the name of making life easier. (For whom? For the parents, the surgeons, or the infants concerned?)

If gender precedes sex, instead of sex preceding gender, then gender is no mere overlay, superimposed upon a pre-existing structure that is still discrete, and that we can still call 'sex' – as if sex had some autonomy from all the social prescriptions within which we ensconce it. Gender, rather, is the way that we organize sex. In the beginning, as it were, was the word. The law of gender dictates how we see sex – there is no 'outside' of culture in or on which we can stand as pre-cultural subjects, a position from which we can construe bodies as if they were somehow in and of themselves outside the cultural matrix within whose terms we configure them. Our preconceptions about gender predetermine how we envisage sex. The science of biology, and the medical establishment, are culturally loaded with presuppositions (given their practitioners, their ideological commitments, and the privileged nature of their collective standpoints), which tell us what sex must be – and what it must not be. Ontologies flourish on the basis of political edicts – such as it ever was. Ontology borrows its authority from its prevailing political commitments, and not the other way around. Aristotle justifies slavery not because he was a bad person, but because, as Marx points out, the commodity form had not become universalized, it had not reached the point of becoming a generalized way of life. This historical argument has its limitations, as we know, since Aristotle's teacher, Plato, was able to argue against gendered customs, to see that women could be philosopher kings or guardians too. Admittedly, as Spelman (1988), and others, have pointed out, Plato's purview was limited to the wives of philosopher-guardians, and had quite a few problems (to put it mildly) when it came to class and 'other considerations' such as race – but you can't have everything all at once, especially in Athens. The point is that Marx's historical exoneration of Aristotle – and he attests, of course, to Aristotle's genius, even as he exonerates him – only works up to a point. That Aristotle could not see that which could only be seen once the commodity form of production universalized itself is a bit of a cop out. If Plato could 'see' that women (of a certain class, and if married to husbands who were philosopher-kings) could be rulers on a par with men, and if J. S. Mill could 'see' in 1869 that women's oppression was a serious philosophical problem long before others were prepared to 'see' these fundamental truths, if Rosa Parks, a humble seamstress, could 'see' that segregation could no longer be accepted in 1955, do we not have to attribute the profundity of these 'seers' to something other than the historical possibilities of their times? Do we not have to grant something to the courage of the convictions of exceptional activists, and thinkers, individuals who took a stand, whose prescience and wisdom enabled them to somehow overcome the barriers that blinded their cohorts, allowing them, as we say, to be 'ahead of their time'?

Let's get back to Calhoun, and the parallel structure she borrows and adopts from Hartmann, reorienting it in a way that at the same time betrays its hegemonic overtones, even if Calhoun does not develop their implications as far as she might. The image of marriage that Hartmann uses, and Calhoun reinvents, as the quest for a potentially healthier relationship between Marxism and feminism calls on us to think about the heterosexist overtones of that image. Calhoun's point is that feminists such as Wittig and Butler have remained blind to an important distinction, namely that between heterosexism and patriarchy. In holding up the lesbian – a runaway slave (an image replete with its own blindness to the specificity of race), an escapee from patriarchy – as the exemplar feminist, Wittig fails to acknowledge that her own conception of lesbian sexuality falls prey to the very patriarchal ideals from which she seeks to escape. For a lesbian, not to be in a subservient relationship with a man is not particularly freeing. Lesbians continue to be the target of institutionalized heterosexism, in its apparent infinite variety of forms, including exclusion from marriage (notwithstanding Butler's critique), the denial of partners' health benefits, discrimination in the workplace at the hands of employers and workmates (in subtle or overt variants), and a host of other insults, affronts, and legislated forms of homophobic anxiety including life-transforming barriers, inhibiting the capacity to adopt children.

Calhoun argues that to construe lesbians as going beyond, bringing into question, or destroying the patriarchal category of 'woman' on the basis of the fact that their opting out of a heterosexual relationship of subservience (doing the dishes, having kids, keeping house – all for a man) is to adopt a peculiarly heterosexist standpoint. Since it never occurred to most lesbians to be conventional housewives in conventional heterosexual relationships of marriage, the fact that they choose not to be implicated in such relationships can hardly be seen as a refusal of its heterosexist connotations. Rather, being a lesbian is a matter of desire. It is a matter of loving other women, being sexually active with other women, defining oneself as attracted to other women. It is not a matter of running away from heterosexual relationships, as if to do so were to overcome patriarchy. Therein lies the problem – the conflation of heterosexism (to which lesbians are subject, just as much – if not more in some instances – as straight people) with patriarchy. Just as Hartmann works hard to separate out feminism from Marxism, in order to show its dynamic is irreducible to that of Marxism, in order to preserve the integrity of gender as distinct from class, so Calhoun carefully and patiently separates out heterosexism from patriarchy. We have learned – and we have learned our lesson well – that patriarchy is not an all embracing structure, covering all instances of sexual relationships (see Rubin 1975). It is not a universal organizing structure, true for all time and all places. It is rather a highly specific structure concerning the power of the father to confer on his children his name, and, as Engels has demonstrated, its monogamous overtones are bound to the desire to have one's own, proper, children, inherit one's property (Engels 1985). Be that as it may, practically everyone continues to use the term patriarchy, Rubin's correct protests notwithstanding, and so will I, until someone comes up with a better term. In any case, such is the global reach of post-industrialist, postcolonialist, individualist capitalist ideology these days, there hardly exist any parts of the world which capitalism, hand in hand with patriarchy, has not invaded. Maybe there are some shreds of matriarchal societies still around, but we've done our level best to destroy their significance (native American matriarchal authority comes to mind, once again), so maybe we should just live with the symbolic consequences.

Calhoun points out, quite rightly, that Wittig and Butler conflate heterosexism and patriarchy. As far as Wittig's argument is concerned, this is pretty clear. Wittig argues that lesbians defy the patriarchal definition of what it means to be a woman, the implication being that the only way to be a true feminist is to be a lesbian. Celibate women, single mothers, and heterosexual women who endeavor to, and sometimes succeed, in making their relationships egalitarian might have something to say about this. Quite apart from that, as we have seen, even if lesbians avoid being in subservient personal relationships with men, they do not avoid the wider structural, societal, heterosexist norms that continue to subject them to the most egregious discrimination. Even as media representations of lesbian and gay lifestyles proliferate, these representations continue to tame and marginalize lesbian or gay couples, finding ways of rendering them safe and innocuous by subordinating them again and again to the straight norm, even while allowing them some airplay. As long as they stay in their place and agree to be non-threatening and non-combative, like the guys who are a virtual advertisement for middle-class, yuppie versions of capitalist aspirations, for example, in *Queer Eye for the Straight Guy*. Four gay men run around a straight guy to give him the 'style' for which gay men are proverbially known, only to enhance his chances of getting his girl, and securing her with matrimonial ties (see Roelofs 2004). The message is: it is okay to be gay, as long as gays work for the hegemony of straight life. We might have come a long way from the history that the likes of Quentin Crisp and Whoopi Goldberg narrate in the film version of Russo's *The Celluloid Closet* (1987), the good old days when men were men and gays were cissies, but we still have a long way to go before lesbians and gays do not just play the token, obligatory, supporting, best friend of the cool, very heterosexual blonde protagonist at the center of the story, waiting for her real, and very hetero man to come along and sweep her off her feet.

In the case of Butler, as per usual, things are a little more complex. Butler has famously argued that gender is drag, that the only way to reinvent gender norms is not to simply turn our backs on them, but to reinvent them, breathing new life into them with our performative citations of gender norms, which parodically and strategically reinvent and reappropriate them. 'I like my boys to be girls' as Butler says. The very transgression of a woman's body miming masculinity is a site of subversion. Butler thus departs from the standard

47

feminist critique of butch/femme relations, whereby feminists complain that to inhabit the roles of butch/femme is merely to replicate patriarchal relations. For Butler, the point is that in resignifying the apparently 'natural' continuity between male bodies, masculinity, and heterosexual desire, butch/femme lesbian relations do not merely replicate in slightly different ways male/female heterosexual relations. Rather, they re-constitute these relationships, mixing up the categories, and playing havoc with the causal relationships generally assumed to underlie the heteronormative signifying chain that lines up male bodies with masculinity, and projects the objects of desire of such masculine/male bodies as pretty, young blondes, with big breasts and thin legs. To be a butch or a femme lesbian is to mess with the signifying system of heteronormative desire. So far, so good. To get to Calhoun's critique. For Calhoun, Butler's repudiation of the feminist critique only gets her so far. It does very little to contest the causal connection between masculinity and power. Butch lesbians can parodically (and sometimes not so parodically) mimic heterosexual male/masculine power by occupying similar symbolic positions, but the normative link between masculinity and power is left untouched, in place, and stronger than ever. It has even recruited new advocates – they might not have the traditional body type, but they do all the other things right, and sometimes even better than 'biological' men. After all, they have all that chic going for them, which even gay men fall for.

Calhoun, one has to admit, has a point. Her point is that Butler and Wittig have failed to distinguish between the heteronormative order and patriarchy (although in some of Butler's later work, I think that such a distinction – and perhaps it is developed partly in response to critiques such as Calhoun's – can be found). Not that Calhoun gets it all right – far from it. Ironically, her analytical clarity, her persuasive logic, and her penchant for preserving parallels even as she adumbrates the differences between patriarchy and heterosexism, show up the limitations of her strategy. Preserving Hartmann as her model, Calhoun capitalizes on the moribund image of a soured marriage by taking the image and reinventing it. Now we have a failed 'marriage,' replete with all the heterosexism of that image, between feminism and lesbian theory. For Hartmann the issue was that Marxism subsumes feminism, that Marxism and feminism are one, and that one is Marxism. For Wittig the issue is that feminist theory subsumes lesbian theory, that feminist and lesbian theory are one, and that one is feminism. Heterosexism wins the day. Not only that, but Calhoun repeats, without taking any critical distance from it, Wittig's problematic, in her implicit parallel between slaves and lesbians. If lesbians are 'runaway slaves,' who are the masters from whom they have run? Patriarchy might be pernicious in many of its aspects, but it does not directly constitute a system of forced labor that dehumanizes and delegitimates its subjects. One has to be a little careful, therefore, in proliferating analogies that cover up more than they reveal, by ignorantly and casually drawing on implied parallels that have not been thought through, and which rely on a wholesale repression of colonial relationships and the histories of slavery that have structured them. This problem is particularly glaring, given the fact that Wittig draws upon Guillamin, who does indeed explore the intricacies of race, only to conveniently forget that race is a problem in its own right, and not one that can be subsumed by feminism, or lesbianism, or any other ism.

If Hartmann, Rubin, and others do a good job of explaining the limitations of any paradigm that assumes that Marxism is the dominant force, and feminism can only ever be second best, a subordinate partner, they are not so clued in when it comes to race. Linda Lim (1983) and Mohanty (1997) correct this neglect of the multinational face of globalized, transnational, imperialist, capitalism. Lim provides an analysis that argues for the need to take on board not just capitalism, and not just patriarchy, but also imperialism. Without doing so, one cannot account for the predominantly exploitative capitalist relations that structure the expansion of developed nations such as Japan, the United States, and those in Western Europe into areas such as South Asia. One cannot explain why third world women workers for Disney's multinationals in Haiti are paid less than it costs to feed their families, why they are paid less than their male counterparts in their own countries, and less than both men and women in western countries for the same work. It is not just that women are exploited by capitalism and patriarchy as intersecting systems in ways that Marxism remains blind to; it is also that racialized women (and men) are exploited by capitalism as it intersects with patriarchy and imperialism, in ways to which white, mainstream, vaguely Marxist feminists remain blind.

We have spent some time seeing how Hartmann parses out the relationship between feminism and Marxism, insisting that the one must not remain circumscribed by the other, and how Calhoun illuminates the discrete systems of oppression that constitute patriarchy on the one hand and heterosexism on the other. Both Hartmann and Calhoun, for all their acumen in analyzing intersecting systems of oppression that deserve to be analytically separated from one another, fail to carry through their insights in order to elucidate the dynamic of imperialism, racism, or nationalism. It is left to Lim, Mohanty, and Uma Narayan to explore the ways in which capitalism and patriarchy support and are supported by imperialist policies, and how problems of anti-colonial nationalism can exacerbate the oppression of third world women, whose bodies often become the sites on which competing narratives about colonialism are played out. Women have often been required to play the roles of repositories of all that is ostensibly good, pure, and sacrosanct about a particular nationalist culture. Tied in with the expectation that their primary role be that of childbearers and homemakers is the probability that not only will women become the dumping ground for patriarchal discontent when they attempt to break out of these roles, but they will also stand accused of being co-opted by 'western,' feminist ideas.

According to the anti-colonial logic that Fanon has traced, and that Narayan has augmented in a feminist direction, patriarchal nationalists, for example, create myths of nationalism which themselves are constructed reactively in relation to colonial myths of nationalism. Selectively narrating anti-colonial versions of nationalism, postcolonial narrators construct their nations in reaction to the alleged corruption of the west, by asserting their spirituality in atavistic terms, and then commandeering women to be representative of the spiritual nation, confining them to the hearth and home that was conventionally the domain of women.

Here, then, is the problem we have been leading up to for a while now. The proliferation of parallels (Marxism and feminism, feminism and lesbian theory, feminism and race theory) which are themselves called into being in attempts to combat the hegemony of systems of oppression (capitalism and patriarchy, patriarchy and heterosexism, patriarchy and imperialism) helps to bring to light discrete problems around the issues of class, gender, and race. Yet for all the power of the proliferation of these analytic categories, the push to separate out, to isolate, to render distinct the problems we designate under class theory, gender theory, lesbian theory, race theory – ad infinitum – carries with it the dangers of obfuscation. These systems might have a certain amount of integrity in and of themselves, but they also depend on one another, reinvent one another, implicate one another, bleed into one another, usurp one another, constitute one another. In short, their relationship is very messy, and does not adhere to the neat contours we, as conceptual framers, would like them to. Feminist theorists have tried to acknowledge this problem to some extent with the language of intersectionality, or interlocking oppressions, or hybridity, and so on. Yet each time we try to articulate the discrete logic of race, and claim it interlocks with the discrete logic of class, or gender, or sexuality, or whatever, we are confronted with an apparently irresolvable problem. The very attempt to shed light on one dynamic brings to light the ineluctable problem of its historical implication with another dynamic. Try as we might to separate them out with analytical clarity, we cannot make patriarchy stand alone, without understanding its inevitable, unavoidable, relationship with colonialism. Neither can we comprehend the development of the logic of capital without also attending to that of the colony. Likewise the subordination of women goes hand in hand with that of racial minorities, and so on. To take one example, the myth of the black rapist is a myth that is indebted as much to the white, Victorian ideal of feminine purity – an idealized version of white feminine sexuality that is tied to the capitalist imperative to reproduce a workforce of what we might term, in a Foucauldian nod, docile bodies, as much as it is to its implicit, racialized opposite that Hammonds has analyzed. While black female sexuality is hypervisible, oversexed, pathologized, immoral, and impure, it is so only in contrast to the idealized, white, moral, reproductive, purified image of Victorian female sexuality. The history of slavery, including the sexual access to female slaves that white slave masters assumed to be their right, played an important part in the representation of black women as oversexed, diseased, and profligate. At the same time, events such as the lynching of blacks, as in the story of Emmet Till, for daring to look at a white woman, play their part in the mythologized black man as sexually uncontrollable, savage, uncivilized, primitive, and bestial. These mythologies assume a place of legitimacy in the white imaginary, such that white men raping black female slaves is rendered inadmissible: there is only room for rapists of one color, and that color must be black. There is only room for one color of female purity, and that color must be white. There is only room for one color of paid laborers, and that color must be white.

The complexity of these 'issues' in their historical imbrication is of labyrinthine proportions. On the one hand, analytical clarity is useful, in separating the various strands and insisting on their integrity. On the other hand, it is obfuscating precisely insofar as the urge to separate and distinguish seems so often to be tied to a blindness to history. Hence the emphases of intersectional models tend to reside in the (implicit) need to take apart or put together these different strands, as if they stood in and of themselves outside their mutual implication. The approach often lacks historical perspective, so that not only the particular identity categories that have recently risen to prominence, but identity categories as such, are assumed, rather than thought as a phenomenon that has only arisen relatively recently (see Zita 1998). Models of intersectionality tend to function synchronically, rather than always also diachronically. To understand this, we need to look at Foucault and Kristeva in greater detail.

In the ongoing quest to enhance feminist theory, so that it overcomes its legacy of exclusions and blindspots, feminist theorists have offered a variety of intersectional models. These models are intended to eschew the problems inherited by what Elizabeth Spelman has identified as the 'additive model,' by which she means theories that identify feminist theory with an unanalyzed commitment to white, middle-class, heterosexual normative commitments, and then adopt an add-and-mix approach. The substratum of feminist theory remains unchanged, while other, previously excluded groups of women are invited to join the club, over which white, middle-class, heterosexual women retain control, by dictating the terms of the debate. You too can be feminists, the message is, as long as you abide by our rules, don't get too uppity or unruly, and don't make any demands that challenge our hegemonic model. Embedded in this view is an abstract concession to differences, which espouses a commitment to diversity according to the variously formulated litany of gender, race, class, and sexuality, but which in fact presumes the centrality of gender, and merely adds on the categories of race, class, and sexuality (and, depending on your degree of sensitivity and willingness to remain open to genuine equality, ableism, ageism, etc. – what Butler has aptly referred to as the illimitable, etc.). This model ostensibly presents itself as engaging difference authentically, all the while perpetuating an unspoken allegiance to gender as the organizing concept, and by default construing it as neutral with regard to all the other categories. This results in an implicit specification of those categories as subsidiary to gender. They remain peripheral to the structural essence of feminist theory, their marginal status ultimately confirming their superfluity to the real concerns of feminists.

In order to move beyond the patronizing discourse, which the old guard of feminists labored under, misconceptions of imperialism, heterosexism, classism, racism, and so on, feminist theorists such as bell hooks, Angela Davis, and Crenshaw (1992), challenged the additive model. They demanded to own their place as integral to feminist theory, and refusing to be relegated to the margins of feminist theory, to serve merely as the experiential examples of white feminist dogmatism, handmaidens to a feminist theory that could assuage its white liberal guilt by agreeing to include a few minority experiences in order to add the flavor of diversity to its theories, but with no real commitment to listening to these marginal voices, or learning from them, or agreeing to transform the hegemonic processes by which dominant voices gain and maintain legitimacy. Certain women of color were admitted into the literary canon, Toni Morrison for example, but the ramifications of their contributions were contained, for the most part, within literary theory, and not allowed to disrupt the Eurocentric theoretical assumptions of white feminist theory, which continued to trace its origins to, and stipulate its theories in terms of, social contract theory, even as it challenged its traditional parameters (Carole Pateman 1988). Even when concessions were made, and black, Latina, and Asian feminist thinkers began to find a forum within the echelons of feminist theory, a certain fetishization characterized their reception. Repeating, with a slightly different twist, the trope whereby a few select, minority voices were granted access to the hallowed halls of academe, so that all of a sudden Kate Chopin's *Awakening* (1976) seemed to be appear on every vaguely feminist literary syllabus, Gloria Anzaldúa (1990) rose to fame, as it apparently became obligatory to cite her – and often only her – as exemplary of the need to take into account 'other' voices in every feminist paper. A few women of color had made it – wasn't that enough? We didn't want them to take over . . . the othering of feminist philosophy must only be allowed to go so far.

bell hooks advocated an interlocking model, and Iris Marion Young wrote a book called *Intersecting Voices* (1997). The idea was to resist the continued hegemony of white, mainstream feminism, to achieve a genuine transformation of feminist theory, which could not be allowed to repeat unthinkingly the problems of its previous incarnation. What did intersectionality mean, and how did it move us beyond the additive model? If race and class could not be adequately theorized on the model of 1 plus 1 plus 1 equals . . . 1 (race plus class plus gender equals a better concept of gender), how did an intersectional model help push beyond this circularity? One implication of the intersectional model is that these categories did not have equal weight for everyone, and that we cannot unproblematically assume their equivalence, such that there is a common form of conceptual exchange to which they are all ultimately reducible. Race for a white person in imperialist, white western countries will not be lived as a problem, but will rather function as an unacknowledged privilege, while race for a black woman, a third world woman, an Asian-American woman, or a Latina woman, will as often as not constitute a barrier, as grounds for discrimination or exclusion. This asymmetrical relationship between racialized experiences will help to inform and shape how gender is lived in a way that is irreducible to any attempt to compartmentalize gender and race. To ask a black, working-class lesbian if she is more oppressed by her race, sexuality, gender, or class is not only to misconstrue the problem – as if a quantitative determination of the relative importance of these factors, even if it were possible to achieve, would solve anything – it is also to commit the error of assuming that the categories of race, gender, sexuality, and class were somehow commensurable with one another. Once we understand, however, that in even apparently liberatory feminist discourses (liberatory for who?) these categories have functioned exclusively, perpetuating and reinventing racism, we must also concede that part of what gender itself has become, as a site around which feminists have rallied, is itself infected by racism. Take the history of civil rights, for example, which suggests that the effects of power tend to be variegated, often along racialized lines, so that both Hegelian and Foucauldian models of power are in operation at the same time for different groups. Civil rights have operated in largely liberatory ways for white, western women, and in this sense power is not just something we oppose but also something we draw on for our regimes of intelligibility, something we depend on for our very existence. Yet they have operated in negative and repressive ways for native American women, whose forced assimilation to American, individualist, capitalist, and colonialist practices has all but obliterated the collective, tribal, traditional ways of life that existed prior to colonization. Far from having been vital to the self-understanding of native American women, or liberatory and empowering, the imposition of American civil rights has proved to be stultifying, prohibitive, and discriminatory. The Hegelian and the Foucauldian models both still seem to be around, but one has more pertinence than the other, depending on the color of your skin. This suggests that the model of power assumed by classic, liberatory discourses has not only blinded those discourses to the unequal distribution of power between racialized groups, but has also actively constituted the concerns of some women as not merely peripheral but antagonistic to the central claims of feminism. Women whose experiences have been constituted through their colonial subjugation, forced relocation, and sterilization, and the erasure of traditional tribal practices and philosophies, have not experienced civil rights as liberating but as oppressive and repressive. Only certain groups of women might well benefit from the discourse of civil rights, replete with its individualist, capitalist, colonialist legacy, in which rights are construed as that which a government confers upon its citizens, the preservation of which the separation of powers is designed to protect. The sphere of the civil state protects the rights of some (typically those of white, European origin) at the cost of eradicating the very way of life of others (native American tribes, Africans transported to the new Americas in order to work as slaves, undocumented immigrants who work for less than the minimum wage, without health benefits or job security).

CHAPTER 3

DISCIPLINING, CONTROLLING, AND NORMALIZING FEMALE SEXUALITY WITH FOUCAULT AND FEMINIST FRIENDS: DOCILE AND RESISTANT BODIES

Influenced by Foucault, and drawing on a suggestion of the Foucauldian theorist David Halperin – namely that the category of homosexuality as we think of it today is inapplicable to ancient Greek society – Jacqueline Zita distinguishes between premodern, modern, and postmodern approaches to sexuality. In the contemporary, postindustrial, advanced capitalist, individualist epoch, as Foucault has shown, sexuality comes to function as a truth about ourselves. Yet such truths could not emerge before the atomistic, individualist notion of the self as decisively distinct from the social nexus definitive of subjectivity – whether this nexus be understood as the feudal system that preceded capitalism, in which serfs were beholden, through a complex system of tithes and obligations, to the lord of the manor, or whether it be at work in the social codes of honor characteristic of life in the polis.

In Plato's *Symposium*, having dismissed the flute girls, Socrates discusses with his male interlocutors the nature of eros, while at the same time a series of homoerotic relations are enacted, through innuendo, word play and overt references (Plato 1975). This tells us something about the way in which male to male homosexuality – far from constituting deviant behavior – in fact operated merely as just one, not particularly stigmatized, mode of manifesting sexuality, among others. Halperin (1990) argues that in ancient Greek society sexual relationships function in a world that establishes social honor in relation to kinship structures, rather than parsing out sexuality in relation to modern, individualist identity categories.

Foucault traces the shift that occurs in the definition of sexuality in the modern period, that of the post-Cartesian era in philosophy. If, within the religious worldview of Christendom, homosexuals were deemed by the priest in the confessional box to be sinners, with the increasing secularization of society the authority of the church passed to that of the medical profession. The medical expert emerged as the one who knows the truth about sexuality, the one who defines certain forms of sexuality as deviant. With this shift from the definition of sexuality away from sin and towards pathology, we also see the emergence of the conditions necessary for modern identity categories to be conceived as political rallying points, around which gays and lesbians began to organize themselves in protest against their marginalization. Gay pride marches established homosexual identity as something to be proud of, rather than as something that should be hidden away. 'We're here, we're queer – get used to it!' This reclaiming of queer identities, the insistence that homosexuality should not be seen as deviant – either as sinful or as pathological – challenged the DSM (Diagnostic and Statistical Manual of Mental Disorders) definition of homosexuality as a pathology.

For Foucault, power in the modern world does not operate simply from the top down, in a monolithic and unidirectional manner. Unlike the power of the monarch, in whose person is vested the ability to punish subjects who fail to obey the rules, the new conception of power that Foucault describes consists in various techniques whereby we administer our bodies and our selves in accordance with disciplinary procedures and expectations, which are not so much imposed from above, as produced from below. The exercise of power is not just negative, prohibitive, or repressive, but also productive of knowledge. It sets up subjects as available for restructuring and disciplining in accordance with regulatory functions of societal norms. Taking over the expertise in which they are trained, individuals are enabled by various technologies of the self to take on the operation of power themselves. The location of power is difficult to discern: it is everywhere and nowhere. Its operation is diffuse, dispersed, anonymous, and bureaucratic. In answer to the question, who is the disciplinarian, we could equally respond on the one hand that it is the subject, who conforms to social dictates, or on the other hand, the media, educators, and social mechanisms that promulgate normative fictions to which subjects respond and with which we engage. Foucault's appeal to the Panopticon, in his investigation into the history of penitentiaries, makes it clear that, just like the prisoners who assume they are under surveillance, and act accordingly, the subjects of modern society take over the role of policing themselves. The effect of the architecture of prisons, schools, and hospitals is to 'induce . . . a state of conscious and permanent visibility that assures the automatic functioning of power' (Foucault 1977, 201). In a parallel way, through the apparatus of media, the male gaze is internalized, as women's fashion magazines and Internet advertisements instruct women with the aim of promoting their 'individuality.' The website UdefineU provides powerful techniques in their self-instruction videos for Posture & Poise, Voice & Speech, Etiquette & Style. The fashion video teaches the fundamental 'rules' of fashion:

- how to organize your closet
- 6 basic pieces every woman should own
- how to shop for them to fit your body type
- what fabrics to pick in terms of feel and cut
- how you can combine these outfits so you can dress for any occasion (whether a date, picnic, work, etc.)

Handing over to us the tools of the trade, companies instruct us on how to perfect our make-up routines, and how to adapt them for every occasion. The make-up experts at féhairandbeauty.com offer advice on 'bridal make up,' and techniques for emphasizing or disguising any particular features of the face. They will 'show you what works best with your personality,' while preparing the market for the next generation of consumers ('bring your children along for any face painting needs they might have,' says féhairandbeauty.com!) Providing step-by-step instructions on everything from washing hair to speaking with the appropriate feminine effect, videos and advertisements inculcate in us the appropriate behavior. Feminine.co.uk describes its eyeliner as 'eternally feminine and seriously seductive,' offering a step-by-step guide as to its application, and instructing us on the necessity of daytime and evening make-up regimes.

The expert vacates his or her proper place, and hands over his or her expertise to the individual themselves, training them to perfect their knowledge in the technique of the correct application of make-up, the appropriate choice of fashion for their figure, and the right haircut for their face. Advertisements are allegedly directed towards individuality, while in fact promoting a stereotypical norm. We become obedient servants of patriarchal norms of feminine beauty, as we train our docile bodies according to the latest techniques of fashion. There has been an explosion of reality TV programs, including *Queer Eye for the Straight Guy*, *What not to Wear*, and extreme makeover scenarios, in which not only is the proper lifestyle and fashion sense instilled in individuals in order to enhance their chances of attracting and keeping the right man or girl, but also the body itself is reformed and, sometimes, quite literally, reshaped – through surgical intervention (liposuction, breast augmentation, nose jobs, etc.). Women are constantly exhorted to reveal their femininity, not to dress in a masculine way, not to hide their figures, not to dress in a fashion that is too young or too old, too tight or too baggy, to dress in a way that is sexy and not frumpy, to show just the right amount of cleavage, to show not too much, but enough leg, to cover up those body parts that show signs of aging, and to make the best of those body parts that still pass as youthful. Women are encouraged to wear high heels, trained to apply make-up in the right way, broken down, often to the point of tears, until they realize the error of their ways, are ready to be enlightened, built up again, and reshaped into willing, pliable fashion plates, onto whose bodies are inscribed the message of patriarchal, heterosexual, normative sexuality. Look like the woman that you are! Allow your inner self to emerge! Develop your true, feminine, sexuality! Free yourself of . . . your own idiosyncratic approach to life, and become like everyone else, dedicated to embodying socially reproduced norms of beauty and acceptability. Step out of the bonds of mediocrity, and into the normative paths of 'sexiness' and femininity. Conform to the expectations of society. Become like all the rest of us . . . isn't this what Beauvoir meant in 1949 when she remarked on the myth of the eternal feminine? 'Becoming a woman,' as one Internet advertisement puts it, means learning what kind of shampoo to buy.

In Sandra Lee Bartky's words, 'no one is marched off for electrolysis at the end of a rifle, nor can we fail to appreciate the initiative and ingenuity displayed by countless women in an attempt to master the rituals of beauty,' but in this mastery women are turned into 'docile and compliant companions of men just as surely as the army aims to turn its raw recruits into soldiers' (1990, 75). If women are trained just as meticulously in the regimes of femininity as men are to manage rifles, what is to be said about the women who increasingly populate the military? Equally, glamour products are progressively aimed at men, who are not only encouraged to try Rogaine and teeth-whitening products, but also to buy skin-care products and strawberry and avocado hair conditioners. This does not obviate the fact that women are still expected to spend a great deal more time than men on their appearance, and that if they don't, they are considered to have 'let themselves go,' whereas men get away with rumpled clothes and uncombed hair by adopting that hapless, masculine stance.

We invest ourselves with patriarchal norms of femininity, adhering to and reproducing culturally specific ideals, disciplining our bodies in order to conform to them. At the same time, we are confronted with those norms of ideal femininity as if they stood over against us, and were unattainable. We will never be as perfect, graceful, and effortlessly feminine as the air-brushed images of supermodels whose photographs compel us to try to live up to the unattainable and artificial ideals they represent. In our efforts to do so, the effects of patriarchal power manifest themselves in the intimate details of the way we live our lives. Power, then, resides in us, in our gestures, mannerisms, corporeal motility, in the ways we walk, dress, and negotiate the world (see Young 2005). Yet at the same time it is invested in the advertisements, films, magazine images, and billboards, in the disciplinary authorities (schools, families, peer groups) which insist on gendering girls and boys according to the conventional, received wisdom of heterosexual dimorphism.

The shift in the model of power Foucault traces moves us away from a totalizing account, and towards a more nuanced, variegated, local analysis, resulting in a micro-political anatomy of sometimes conflicting forces. It is not just a matter of pledging allegiance to a monarch, nor even a matter of the forces of capitalism appropriating the products of labor. This new relation is much more personal, much more bodily, and much more invasive. It is no longer simply the capitalist who owns the means of production and governs ideology, while the proletariat is the subjugated victim of oppression, without resources except those granted by the oppressor. Nor is it just the products of our labor that are the result of the commodity form of production. Control extends to the operation of our daily lives, and exerts its influence in microscopic detail over every aspect of our person. Power is more invasive and its effects more insidious. In fact, as Deleuze points out, although Foucault has been widely understood to have focused on a disciplinary society, he sees the twentieth century less in terms of discipline, and more in terms of control (Deleuze 1995, 174–5). It is not so much a model of confinement, as in the prison, school, or hospital model of the Panoption, rather it is a matter of constant monitoring, instant communication, and relentless, invasive advertising, junk emails, and spam. We cannot enjoy the privacy of our own home computers without being bombarded with an unsolicited array of demands in the form of pop-up windows that sometimes, no matter what you try, will not go away. In more Deleuzian than Foucauldian terms, we might say that the cyber, information, or computer age is an age in which the machine-body is held out as an ideal for us, an ideal for us to emulate, to take over, to become. An advertisement for the Atkins diet informs us that 'we have the information to turn your body into a healthy weight loss fat-burning machine!' It is not only the products of laborers, but our bodies themselves that are commandeered. True to Foucault's analysis, it is knowledge that will enable our bodies to become fat-burning machines, and it is information that will set us free.

Seeping down into the very capilliaries of our bodies, power is multiple, situational, relational, strategic, and variegated. Power is everywhere, in pockets of resistance, as well as in repressive policies. In some respects, a group might be powerless, while in other respects, its power is exerted, whether this power is turned against its erstwhile oppressors, or whether it is turned against another convenient target. Rather than the 'us' and 'them' model, where there is a clear oppressor and a clear victim, where one party unambiguously has all the power, and the other has none, recognizing the multiplicity of power makes it possible to acknowledge that there are no clear, outright winners or losers. A white woman might be repressed by the demands of patriarchy, but she herself might also exercise a racialized form of power over other women, for example. Indeed she might, consciously or unconsciously, invoke patriarchal conventions in order to strategically set herself against minority women, aligning herself with white, patriarchal power structures in the process.

If Foucault recognizes at the theoretical level the multiple strategies of power that constitute its networks, he leaves it to others to address how, for example, ideals of femininity are specifically taken up in the production of docile bodies. If, at some level, women are constituted by the repressive expectations of normative femininity, at another level women constitute themselves as wielding power by mastering the skills that enable them to embody or approximate the ideal of white, heterosexual, femininity. As Bartky points out, women might experience feminism as threatening, insofar as it challenges women's conformity with received ideals, prompting a process of 'deskilling.' Women experience feminists who criticize beauty parades and distance themselves from conventional norms of femininity as undermining them and the skills they have worked so hard to acquire and embody.

Bartky does a wonderful job of expanding Foucault's analysis so that it applies to the gendered subject of femininity, illustrating the minute disciplining of the female body as it occurs through exercise, diet, fashion, and make-up regimes. The production of femininity is accomplished through a vast array of disciplinary regimes, which regulate appearance, body shape, size, configuration, and ornamentation. Bartky expertly adumbrates the sometimes painful and expensive techniques by which women are exhorted to become appropriately feminine women, from getting rid of body hair, through the use of waxing, or depilatory creams, to painting the face according to a partitioning of the day into daytime and evening make-up regimes. Emphasizing individualized attention and the technological aspect of feminine disciplines of the body, the National Skin Institute promises that 'it all comes down to management,' that 'We can help you manage your unwanted hair' by starting 'a plan that's just right for you,' and adds 'We have . . . the most advanced technologies.' Just as Foucault had elaborated on the disciplinary mechanisms through which schools operated, partitioning the schoolchildren's day into minute segments of time, and the architectural space into appropriate places for each activity (reading, writing, eating), Bartky draws our attention to the rules and regulations that demand women utilize space and time in ways that ensure the appropriate gait, swinging of hips, ways of getting in and out of cars, with maximum efficiency and effect.

Given Foucault's theoretical appreciation of the fact that far from being univocal, conceptions of power vary from one historical epoch to another, with new discourses manifesting the multiplicity and instability of power, its operation as a network, and its nature as relational and strategic, one might argue that the logical implications of a feminist appropriation of a Foucauldian conception of power would be to elaborate the tensions characteristic of its conflicting and confrontational operation. If the operation of power is to be characterized as multidirectional, one approach, which Foucault himself refrained from developing, but which theorists such as Hammonds (1997) have pursued, is to ask how discourses of sexuality have operated differentially for women, along the lines of race, class, and sexuality. If the Victorian repressive motif of purity, modesty, and chastity was upheld for, and imbibed by, white, middle-class, heterosexual women, the sexuality of African-American women was understood in opposition to such an ideal. Organized around the other pole of a binary opposition, African-American sexuality has been represented as immoral, impure, diseased, and pathologized. Black women have been hypersexualized – witness Saarjite Baartman – and at the same time rendered invisible. In reaction to the hyperbolic representations of black female sexuality perpetuated by Eurocentric myths, those black women who have gained access to the academy, who have become producers of knowledge, are reluctant to draw attention to their anatomy, which has served the white imaginary only as a site of denigration. Given the 'politics of silence' that has been produced along the historical contours of racial contestation, replete with its history of slavery, it is perhaps unsurprising that some black women, particularly lesbians, have found themselves subject to policing by other black women – typically heterosexual, middle-class women. Already marked as deviant in relation to white women, black women are loathe to accept, or identify with, forms of sexuality that are liable to mark them as doubly deviant. There is a dearth of theoretical and historical analyses of black female sexuality precisely because the bodies of black women have so often been represented in exaggerated ways by a white imaginary that is not made accountable for its racist representations. The understandable, if regrettable, reactive response by black women theorists has been to keep quiet about black, female, sexuality, a silence that Hammonds and others have begun to break.

As Gayatri Chakravorty Spivak (1988) has famously argued, for all Foucault's undoubted brilliance, he does not take on the global aspects of capitalism, or the racial significance of the international division of labor. To take seriously the fact that western ways of life are reliant on exploitation of third world labor, especially third world female labor, in the form of subcontracting and multinational exploitation, and severe penalties for worker organization, is to suggest that while the capitalist mode of organization might have transmogrified into new models of power for white, privileged groups in the west, it is still very much alive elsewhere. Whether occupying the ranks of peasant insurgencies in colonial India, or inadequately paid female workers in multinational clothing corporations, whose jobs and livelihoods are jeopardized if they dare to speak out against their extreme poverty and subjugation, the subaltern is very much circumscribed by a totalizing mode of power. This suggests a differential analysis along racialized lines. Hammonds implicitly reworks

63

Foucault's reflections on the repressive hypothesis in the *History of Sexuality* by suggesting that the norms of purity and Victorian respectability could only be upheld by women for whom the invisible norm of whiteness functioned to separate their own sexuality from the characterization of black, female sexuality as degenerate. Similarly, it could be argued that there are differential models of power for the first and third worlds.

For all the explanatory power and virtuosity of Bartky's analysis, which, judging from the consistent reaction of students in my feminist theory classes, is considerable, she does not allow for any sustained consideration of how race, class, and sexuality configure bodies differently. She falls into the trap of either insisting that femininity operates similarly across race, class, or sexuality – a model that confirms gender as the bedrock of feminist analysis, while treating race, class, and sexuality as just so many additional, peripheral, secondary factors – or of attempting to specify the special circumstances of class or sexuality in a way that draws on stereotypes which do little to advance a serious consideration of how these aspects of identity demand that some of her central claims be rethought. To suggest that working-class women purchase their cosmetics at Wal-Mart, while upper-class women purchase theirs at high-end department stores is at best stereotypical and at worst insulting. While some effort is made to provide an analysis that is inclusive of diverse races and sexualities, Bartky ends up upholding white femininity as an ideal without adequately problematizing that ideal. Skin creams to whiten the skin of African-American women are available, Bartky tells us, illustrating how whiteness is upheld as the norm of beauty, irrespective of race. It is certainly true, as Toni Morrison's *The Bluest Eye* demonstrates admirably, that an ideal of whiteness permeates society such that the idea of having blue eyes captivates Pecola Breedlove, who thinks that if she could only be granted this wish she would embody the ideal of perfect femininity. Yet, isn't there more to say about the disciplining of racialized bodies than this? In the same way that Bartky assumes all lesbians can be characterized as butch, she also assumes that the topic of race is adequately covered by making a few quick references to black women.

To be fair, both feminist analyses and marketing strategies have advanced since Bartky wrote her article in 1990. My point is not to condemn Bartky, far from it – her analysis remains invaluable for its challenge to the limitations of Foucault's gender-blind account, and the incisive way in which she extrapolates some of Foucault's insights to an account of gendered normativity. The question remains, however, in what areas does Bartky's analysis itself remain beholden to holdovers of an essentially mainstream (white, heterosexist, middle-class) feminist analysis? To what extent does Bartky herself import a revised version of Foucauldian universalism, extending her analysis to women's differential relation to power, but failing to differentiate between divergent experiences of women, as if all women were gendered, raced, and classed in essentially the same ways, as if feminism merely needs to tweak its insights in order to be genuinely inclusive? Those of us committed to advancing feminist analyses must take seriously critiques by women of color which justifiably point out that in order for feminism to become genuinely inclusive it is not enough for white feminists to allow 'others' to join 'our' club, so long as we still control the terms of the debate. As a case in point, an organizing category of analysis for Bartky is body size and configuration. Women, we are told, are encouraged to go on diets and exercise regimes in order to maintain slim figures, and women therefore place demands on themselves to shape their bodies accordingly, in order to embody the ideal of femininity. The concept 'women' is intended to apply to all women, irrespective of race. Yet, a closer look at the question of how beauty regimes are marketed to different ethnic groups reveals that the ideal of slimness does not apply across the board, in the same way for all women. An Internet advertisement for hair products aimed at African-American women suggests a discrepancy between the way in which femininity relates to weight issues in white and black communities. 'For a black woman, her whole attitude begins with her hair,' says Jolorie Williams, senior product manager for a hair-care product aimed at African-American women. 'She's going to spend money on her hair because she won't go anywhere unless her hair is done. It's not socially acceptable. She can be overweight but her hair must look good.'

In a Foucauldian vein, perhaps we should be tracing specific genealogies, which articulate the particular forces that have come to bear on the possibilities of rendering visible particular aspects of the experiences peculiar to, for example, historically situated black women. Hammonds shows, in a vaguely Foucauldian analysis, how a 'politics of silence' has been produced around the theme of black women's sexuality, in reaction to the hypervisibility and patholo-gization of black women's sexuality, which has been constructed in contradistinction to the norm of ostensible purity characterizing white women's sexuality. Black women's sexuality has on the one hand been subject to hyperbolic and insistent exposure as deviant, and on the other hand been shrouded in silence, precisely in response to the misrepresentations to which black women have been systematically exposed by white, Eurocentric vision. White ideals of the purity of Victorian femininity emerged as counter to a mythologized black female sexuality as uncontained and uncontrollable. Under these conditions, the difficulty of articulating a black, lesbian politics becomes paramount. Policed by middle-class, heterosexual blacks, black lesbians are discouraged from rendering themselves doubly deviant: not only are they already marginalized according to their alleged oversexed characters, they are further marginalized according to their alleged deviance from heterosexual norms.

Witness Saarjite Baartman, who was paraded around Europe, first in London, and then in Paris, as if she were a monstrosity, a curiosity, a freak in a circus. Finally, her genitalia were put on display in the Musée de l'homme in Paris as an intriguing anatomical specimen, until Nelson Mandela had her bodily remains returned to South Africa, where her body could, finally, be laid to rest in peace. Exposing the hypocrisy underlying the double standards applied to white and black female sexuality, Hammonds' approach makes it possible to excavate the buried history of slavery informing the construction of a binary opposition (black equals oversexed, immoral, impure, while white equals appropriately sexed, tending toward the reproductive ends of capitalism, moral, and pure). The standards of Victorian sexuality were applied to white women, whose sexuality was purified by being applied to socially acceptable ends, while the conditions under which black, female sexuality came to be represented as diseased, immoral, and pathological remain unstated. Under slavery, the rape of African-American women by their white masters occurred almost as a matter of course. Taking Hammonds' analysis in a slightly different direction – not one in which she would necessarily be prepared to go – we could draw on a psychoanalytic vocabulary to account for the processes of denial and repression at work in the attempts of white theorizing to account for the past. By projecting the violence of slavery onto black bodies themselves, making them repositories of all that is unacceptable in themselves, in a denial of their own responsibility, whites could exonerate their own behavior, impose imaginary boundaries separating their own standards of morality from those of blacks, and represent blacks as profligate. Such a dynamic can be illuminated by taking seriously Freud's insistence on the unconscious, and his highlighting of various strategies of denial. Melanie Klein's notion of projective identification, in which infantile strategies intended to defend oneself against anxiety themselves become loaded with destructive potential, has found its way into contemporary psychoanalytic theory (1986). Influenced by Klein's notion of various ways of splitting up both consciousness and the world into good and bad, Julia Kristeva, for example, has explored a similar dynamic under the heading of abjection. At issue in abject processes is a preliminary attempt to separate oneself off from the other, paradigmatically the mother, who is not yet considered as conceptually distinct from the self. A provisional attempt at separation, even before that of consciousness and unconscious, or self and other, abjection is a way of territorializing the world, parceling it out into pockets that are manageable, while disposing of that which falls outside the bounds of the manageable by discarding it as just so much waste. Crucial to this movement is the inherent instability of the incipient borders of abjection, an instability owing to the fact that this process – one way of articulating the semiotic – precedes any conceptual understanding of the ontological separation of subjects, both from one another and from objects. Desire is not yet at stake, and neither are there any easily recognizable boundaries of subjectivity. What is at stake is the dumping of affects across borders, as a reaction to the threat posed by the withdrawal of gratification (absence of the mother/withdrawal of breast), a reaction which also consists in the setting up of tentative boundaries. The drawing up of what will become, but is not yet, me and what will become, but is not yet, you, demarcates the borders of my body, as the child, in effect, declares: this shall be inside me and this shall be outside me, this is good, and this is bad (Freud). Judith Butler has appropriated this projective dynamic to shed light on the way in which gays and lesbians come to figure in the heterosexist imaginary as phobic objects, coming to represent a threat to straight lifestyles, a threat that only functions as meaningful through the foreclosure of certain sexual positions. Phobia is produced by a prior expulsion of fearful sentiments, a rejection that attaches to others via mechanisms of exclusion that do not so much posit as enact homosexuals as unviable subjects who do unnameable things. Sarah Ahmed (2005) has developed a theory of abjection in the context of how communities are structured through the systematic moving away of certain bodies from other bodies, and their moving towards others. She gives a metonymical reading of the processes by which nations set up their boundaries along the lines of color, and according to affects such as disgust. Young (1990) and Oliver and Trigo (2003) have extrapolated the discourse of abjection to other forms of socially exclusionary dynamics such as racism and classism. The issue of abjection is one that will be taken up again, in Chapter 6, in relation to Kristeva. First, however, I want to explore the interventions that feminist theorists have made into the issues of epistemology and science, questions that are related to many of those that Foucauldian feminists have put on the agenda, and to look at postcolonial feminist theory.

CHAPTER 4

FEMINIST EPISTEMOLOGY: SCIENCE, KNOWLEDGE, GENDER, OBJECTIVITY

I want to begin this chapter by re-telling a story that I shall call the story of the hapless monk. The following two pages are heavily indebted to Laqueur (1990).

THE HAPLESS MONK

A young aristocrat, obliged to become a monk because his family came upon hard times, visited a country inn. He found the innkeepers mourning their only daughter, reputed to have been very beautiful. In their distress, the parents of the unfortunate maiden asked the monk to watch over her body through the night, until the burial, which was to take place the next morning. The young monk agreed to do so, and duly took up his appointed place. The night wore on, and the young man grew restless. Curious to verify reports of her great beauty, the monk lifted the shroud that covered the body and found the maiden indeed beautiful even in death. Tempted by his desires, and despite his religious vows, the monk, in the words of the eighteenth-century physician who with delicacy records this story for posterity, 'took the same liberties with the dead that the sacraments of marriage would have permitted in life' (Laqueur 1990, 1). In the morning, overcome by shame, the monk departed without waiting for the funeral.

During the ceremony, as the coffin was being lowered, one of the pall bearers felt movement from inside the coffin. When the lid was removed the young woman was found to be still alive, recovering from what must have been a coma. Still rejoicing in the discovery that their daughter was alive after all, the parents were alarmed to find, in due course, that not only was she alive but also inexplicably pregnant. They resolved to put her in a convent as soon as the child was born.

Time passed, and the young aristocrat's circumstances changed for the better. He returned to the inn on business, and learned the news of the daughter's fate, and what had become of his apparently necrophiliac act. On hearing that she was now in a convent, the young man asked permission to marry her.

Thomas Laqueur, a historian of science, opens his book *Making Sex: Body and Gender from the Greeks to Freud* with this story, recounting three different uses to which the story has been put in medical history. In 1749, Jacques-Jean Bruhier reports the incident to demonstrate the moral that 'only scientific tests can make certain' that someone is 'really dead,' and even 'intimate contact' cannot determine death (Laqueur 1990, 2). A contemporary surgeon, Antoine Louis, offered a second interpretation. He refused to accept that anyone could really have believed the girl to be dead, citing as evidence the fact that the monk seemed to have found her animated enough, and concluding that a cover-up story must have been fabricated by the inkeepers' daughter and the monk. The girl must have feigned the coma until the very last moment, giving up her pretense only when death was imminent. At the time it was believed that conception could not occur without orgasm, and for this reason, the surgeon, Louis, thought that the young woman *must* have given signs of liveliness (Laqueur 1990, 3).

By 1836, the same story was being used as evidence for the view that orgasm was not necessary for conception, but was in fact irrelevant to it. Laqueur goes on to suggest that it was only when the equality of men and women became an issue politically that female sexual organs were recognized as significantly different from those of men (Laqueur 1990, 10). Until that point, female sexual organs were simply considered to be a variant of male sex organs, basically the same, but inverted. Only in 1759 was a detailed representation of the female skeleton produced, presumably because, if we follow Laqueur's thesis about the predominance of what he calls the 'one-sex' model, it was considered unnecessary to independently represent female anatomy in biology textbooks since it was assumed to be essentially the same as male anatomy, albeit upside-down and internal to the body, rather than external and visible (Laqueur 1990, 8, 26–62).

I begin by referring to Laqueur not only because his story of the hapless monk highlights the issues that I want to pursue here – namely the historicity of science, and the role played by interpretation in science – but also because I want to mark the absence of a reading that appears neither among the three different readings offered in the annals of medical history, nor in Laqueur's own commentary. The first lesson to draw from the divergent uses to which this anecdote was applied is that anatomy and politics cannot be neatly separated from one another, as if they occupied two mutually exclusive realms. Laqueur suggests – and his insights are influenced by contemporary feminist writings (Laqueur 1990, ix) – that it was precisely when the equality of the sexes was put on the political agenda that the accurate representation of female anatomy also surfaced as an issue. Here, then, is an example of political interests informing and shaping what qualified as legitimate and worthwhile scientific enquiry. The story illustrates a point that, while it remains controversial, has become rather familiar by now – namely that interpretation plays a role in scientific enquiry. The same facts, read in different ways, support widely divergent views. Initially the facts were used to support the eighteenth-century view that conception requires orgasm, yet in 1836 it could serve as evidence for the argument that orgasm is irrelevant to conception. This divergence casts doubt on the fixity of the scientific object. Both the contradictory purposes the story of the hapless monk served, and the fact that there was a significant shift – between the eighteenth and nineteenth centuries – away from a one-sex model and towards a two-sex model, illustrate that we cannot assume that what constitutes the body, or sex, has boundaries that are fixed in space, stable over time, or immune to social and political change.

Finally – and this is where I want to note the absence of what seems to me a salient observation about this story – none of the commentators, including Laqueur (all of them male) appear to have noticed that since the girl was not dead, whether she was comatose or not, the monk's act qualified not as that of a necrophiliac, but rather as that of a rapist. I cannot help but wonder if the pertinence of this distinction would have escaped comment over the span of nearly three hundred years if one of our commenatators had been a woman. If the difference to which I have pointed did not go unnoticed, but merely unremarked by our male commentators, to what should we attribute their silence? The apparent irrelevance of the distinction? Whether unnoticed or unremarked, the fact remains that the distinction in question was not recorded. Presumably it doesn't count as knowledge.

THE CARTESIAN LEGACY

Philosophers since Plato have become accustomed to distinguishing between knowledge on the one hand and opinion on the other. Those who are enlightened are those who understand the difference between the confused shadows on the cave wall, and the true, eternal, universal ideals that make those images possible in the first place. Fantasy and reality, we philosophers are in the habit of thinking, are realms that are in need of sharp demarcation. Not only is it possible to distinguish rigorously between mere belief and well-founded truth; it is the central task of philosophy to do so. The pursuit of true knowledge represents the undisputed goal of philosophers.

In this post-Cartesian era, we no longer imagine that, in the ignorance of our unfounded opinions, we inhabit an underground cave, a murky state which we must transcend in order to gain access to the forms or ideas in the upper world, the intelligible realm. Acquiring knowledge, as we envisage it now, is a matter of establishing principles of certainty, or indubitable truths, the security of which provides the foundation for building systematic knowledge. It is no longer the Platonic divide that banishes myth and prejudice to the underground realm, separating illusion from reality. It is rather the Cartesian subject's ability to establish, through the *cogito*, a ground of certainty, which provides the basis for knowledge, a knowledge that is acquired by reason and sanctioned by truth. Formulated in this way, the task of the philosopher is to overcome subjective prejudice, and to subdue any flights of fancy by imposing the constraints of reason according to the canons of logic, and in conformity with the demands of objectivity. In order to know the world, which is taken to be external to and independent of the subject, the philosopher must find a reliable method of approaching it, and dependable means for representing it. Accuracy is paramount. The purpose of philosophy is, to use an image that Rorty popularized, to reflect the world, to act as a mirror of nature (Rorty 1986).

Not only does the Cartesian approach assume that reason is the tool that will allow us to gain access to, and knowledge of, the empirical world, thus positing rationality as supreme, it also gives rise to an epistemology that builds upon Plato's distinctions 'between knowledge and opinion, and between appearance and reality' (Rorty 1994, 22), imposing a dualism whose impact is still felt, even as its authority is increasingly brought into question. The dichotomy between object and subject is associated with a series of oppositions, including reason and emotion, facts and values, universality and particularity, necessity and contingency, intellectuality and materiality. It hardly needs to be added that the relationship between objective reason, universals, necessary truths, and facts, on the one hand, and subjective emotions, values, particulars, and contingencies on the other is a hierarchical one that usually functions in favour of objectivity and at the expense of subjectivity. We are, as Rorty puts it in his essay 'Solidarity or Objectivity?':

> heirs of [an] objectivist tradition, which centers around the assumption that we must step outside our community long enough to examine it in the light of something which transcends it. . . . Much of the rhetoric of contemporary intellectual life takes for granted that the goal of scientific enquiry into man is to understand 'underlying structures,' or 'culturally invariant factors,' or 'biologically determined patterns'. . . . (1994, 22)

Several consequences and implications can be drawn from the ideal of objective truth that follows in the wake of our Cartesian legacy, with its meditative, self-reflective starting point. Ideal knowers are assumed to be solitary, atomistic individuals, who strive for a position of neutrality and impartiality with respect to cultural or historical bias. The ideal object of knowledge is assumed to be timeless, unchanging, and ahistorical. The subject is assumed to be the abstract bearer of human rights, and human rights are premised upon universal features of humanity that are cross-national and trans-historical. Subjects are posited as if they were essentially the same, and any differences between individuals are treated as incidental, irrelevant, or contingent to the proper concerns of philosophy. Legitimate philosophical investigation seeks for truths which are taken to be universal, neutral, and impartial.

Among those to have rejected these post-Cartesian assumptions are feminists, who have argued that even scientific knowledge, often seen as embodying the paradigm of objectivity, is not disinterested or impartial, but reflects the interests of its knowers. If knowledge is construed not as a set of facts that are collected independently of the situatedness of the community of knowers, but rather as socially constructed in a significant sense, then it no longer seems appropriate to conceive of knowledge in ahistorical terms. Knowledge is socially situated, not timeless and unchanging. Subjects are not envisaged as essentially identical to one another, but rather as embedded in cultural and social circumstances that constitute them in ways that are irreducible to incidental and contingent factors. Cultural differences, on this account, are not ultimately dismissed as superfluous to the universal similarity of subjects, understood as rational agents. Differences between individuals, the interplay between subjects and their communities, must be factored into philosophical investigation, rather than eliminated as contingent and therefore irrelevant. Once the social and political positioning of individuals within and vis-à-vis their communities is no longer seen merely as information from which philosophical enquiry must abstract, but as constitutive of how knowledge is legitimated as knowledge, then the ideal neutrality, impartiality, and universality of philosophical knowledge must also be questioned. The knowledge/power nexus, as it has come to be called, must be interrogated.

Feminists have isolated several different concerns surrounding the relationship of gender to objectivity: for example, disembodiment and the identity assumed by knowers, the alleged timelessness and universality of truth, the essential fixity and sameness of objects of knowledge, and the neutrality and impartiality of knowledge. I want to pursue some of these issues by addressing two specific areas which are central to philosophical enquiry, and which serve to illustrate how gender has been used by feminists to contest traditional notions of objectivity. After some brief remarks about the mind/body problem, I first explore the question of ethics, and then turn to that of science.

THE ABSENT BODY

Philosophy is taken to be the search for impartial, neutral, and value-free truths, whose import is universal and necessary. The body is taken to be largely irrelevant to philosophy, except insofar as it figures as an encumbrance to knowledge in that our senses tend to mislead us, our emotions detract from the capacity for rational thought, and our desires distract us from the pursuit of the good. If it figures at all, the body is merely a site to be contained, ruled over, and subdued. Abstract and disembodied truths are what philosophy aims for, the validity of which is unimpeded by differences in historical eras, geographical locations, or cultural discrepancies.

If abstract reason is assumed to be the means, and universal truths are taken to be the end of the philosophical enterprise, then there is little room for taking account of cultural norms, religious beliefs, or societal structures. Race, class, and sex are seen as incidental to the metaphysical essence, or the inner core of humanity. They are mere details that carry little weight in the grand scheme of things. They deflect from the task of philosophy, as just so much debris that needs to be cleared away in order to get a clear picture of the objective truths that are assumed to be at the heart of philosophy. Underlying the historical sedimentations that have built up in the form of particular cultural and social formations lies the truth of reality, and it is the task of the philosopher to get at it.

In reaction to the idea that the body is essentially irrelevant to philosophy, feminists have begun to explore embodiment as a relevant site of difference between the sexes. Along with a renewed interest in sexual difference, which is interrogated both by theorists influenced by Lacan, such as Irigaray (1985) and Kristeva, and by object-relations theorists such as Benjamin (1990) and Chodorow (1978), feminist thought has included a reorientation of ethical thinking towards an ethics grounded in maternal thinking (Ruddick 1980), and directed toward an ethics of care (Gilligan 1982; Noddings 1984). One of the principal elements of this orientation is the emphasis on our caring connection with others, over and against the atomistic, essentially solipsistic ideal of the meditative Cartesian thinker. Rather than envisaging a world that is made of (at least potentially) rational knowers, whose connection to other agents has to be forged, and whose duties to others need to be outlined in terms of universals, the care ethic takes as its starting point our embeddedness in relations with others. The networks that constitute our relationships with others inform the way we think not just of others but also of ourselves. Taking seriously our responsibility to others thus also contributes to the very notion of our identities.

AN ETHICS OF CARE

Reason may play a part in our ethical decision making, but it is not necessarily the sole arbiter of ethical choice, nor even always the most important one. In this sense, a rationally explicable world may not be the end that should be assumed by ethical systems, while abstract notions of justice and fairness may not be adequate or appropriate ideals to strive toward. If we assume that in the moral sphere rational agents are essentially – at least potentially – identical to one another, and as knowers they are ideally impartial, then the differences in the social positioning of knowers, which may be informed by factors such as class background, ethnic identity, or gender roles, can play no relevant role in the different processes of reasoning that individuals may follow in responding to ethical problems. Not only are differences between individuals considered irrelevant for the purposes of knowledge, but as a result of abstracting from differential circumstances, some ways of knowing are privileged over others. Rationality has been shaped in large measure according to our Enlightenment heritage, and the values we hold dear derive from ways of knowing that tend to construe reasoning as a process undertaken by rationalist individualist subjects who are disembodied, disinterested, and impartial.

In research popularized by Gilligan, in her controversial book *In a Different Voice*, eleven-year-old Amy responds to a dilemma posed to her about whether or not it is right for a husband to steal medicine he cannot afford for his wife who needs it urgently because her life is in danger. Amy's response is to change the terms of the debate, rather than, like Jake (also eleven years old) accepting the challenge as posed by the interviewer. Jake thinks that Heinz should go ahead and steal the drug to save his wife's life 'because,' in his words, 'life is worth more than money' (Gilligan 1982, 26). Jake's lack of equivocation earns him a higher score on Kohlberg's scale of moral development than Amy. Amy's reaction is to look for an alternative to the stark horns of the dilemma with which she is presented: either Heinz steals, which is illegal, or he allows his wife to die, which is wrong. Amy's answers reveal a tendency to reflect upon the situation as a whole, to think about the consequences of stealing, and the effect it might have upon the family in the future. Kohlberg's assumptions, as Gilligan interprets them, leave little room for seeing Amy's attempt to find another way of resolving the problem by talking it over as anything but 'evasive and unsure' (28). Whereas Jake grasps the distinction between property and life that Kohlberg is looking for, seeing the moral dilemma 'sort of like a math problem with humans' (26 [Jake's words]), and setting it up 'as an equation' for which he produces the right 'solution' (26), Amy's attempt to find an alternative to the dilemma posed to her goes unrecognized, merely earning her a lower score on Kohlberg's scale of values. Amy considers the 'effect that theft could have on the relationship between Heinz and his wife' (28), pointing out that 'If he stole the drug . . . he might have to go to jail, and then his wife might get sick again,' and concluding that 'they should . . . talk it out and find some other way to make the money' (28 [Amy's words]). Gilligan's point is that 'Kohlberg's definition of the stages and sequence of moral development' (30) is biased toward the 'conventions of logic' (29) to which Jake appeals, rather than the 'process of communication' (29) on which Amy relies. Rather than seeing Amy's response as 'an evasion of the dilemma' (31), Gilligan focuses upon the way it 'fall[s] through the sieve of Kohlberg's scoring system' (31).

Drawing out a series of oppositions that distinguish Jake's and Amy's responses, Gilligan regards Jake's judgement as reflecting the 'logic of justice,' and Amy's as demonstrating an 'ethic of care' (30). Amy sees the situation not as a 'hierarch[ical]' (32) 'contest of rights' between 'opponents' (30) which depends upon the 'imagery of winning and losing' (32), but in terms of encouraging 'communication' (1982, 32) between 'members of a network of relationships' (30). For Gilligan, Amy's response is not 'naive and cognitively immature' (30), but represents a 'differen[t] mode of moral understanding' (32).

I said that Gilligan's work has proved controversial. Critics have focused on a variety of problems which concern both the ideological import of Gilligan's message, and the methodological adequacy of her research. Linda Kerber is concerned about the 'historical revisionism' (Kerber et al. 1986, 309) she thinks characterizes Gilligan's argument that 'women define themselves through relationships with others, through a web of relationships of intimacy and care rather than through a hierarchy based on separation and self-fulfillment' (1986, 306). While Kerber finds 'invigorating' Gilligan's 'insistence that behavior once denigrated as waffling, indecisive, and demeaningly "effeminate" ought rather to be valued as complex, constructive, and humane,' (306) she worries that a 'single-minded focus on women's own culture . . . risk[s] . . . ignoring "the larger social and historical developments of which it was a part"' [quotation from Ellen DuBois], and does not address the restraining and confining elements of women's culture (308). Kerber sees Gilligan's insistence upon a different voice as reinscribing and reifying a 'rigid dualism' (308), which ultimately re-enacts the traditional bifurcation of men and women's separate spheres of action, whereby culture ascribes 'reason to men and feeling to women' and 'where men [are] understood to realize themselves best in the public sector . . . and women in domesticity' (306). Kerber agrees that 'our culture has long undervalued nurturance and that when we measure ethical development by norms more attainable by boys than by girls our definition of norms is probably biased,' but she objects to what she sees as Gilligan's emphasis upon 'the biological basis of distinctive behavior' (309).

Greeno and Maccoby argue that 'Gilligan has been attacking a straw man,' citing research by Lawrence Walker showing that 'in childhood and adolescence, there is no trend whatever for males to score at higher levels than females on Kohlberg's scales' and that 'in studies that do show sex differences, the women were less well educated than the men, and it appears that education, not gender, accounts for women's seeming lesser maturity' (Kerber et al. 1986, 312). Zella Luria has reservations about the methodological validity of Gilligan's results, maintaining that 'the nature of the evidence is sometimes unclear,' that she is too reliant on 'the single method of the semi-structured interview,' that her 'sample specification is inadequate to justify her group characterizations,' and that 'samples drawn from classes on moral development at Harvard University are dubious exemplars of students generally' (Kerber et al. 1986, 316–7). According to Luria, Gilligan's book 'lacks any careful statement' of methodological issues (318), and 'contains no statement describing her interview and scoring criteria' (319). By weaving together 'literary examples (presumably as metaphors), theoretical proposal, and loosely defined empirical research' she produces results that may be 'winning' but are also 'seductive' (316). Carol Stack, who has conducted her own research from which she develops an African-American model of moral development, follows up on Luria's methodological critique by pointing out that Gilligan's theory derives 'a female model of moral development from the moral reasoning of primarily white, middle-class women in the United States,' and reminding us that as 'Black and Third World feminist researchers have emphasized gender is a construct shaped by the experience of race, class, culture, caste, and consciousness' (Kerber et al., 1986: 324). (For further criticisms and discussion of Gilligan see Benhabib [1992], Kittay and Meyers [1987], and Sunstein [1990]).

Gilligan's work, and the responses it has elicited, serves to situate many of the tensions that have pervaded feminist discourse, and demonstrates how questions about gender and objectivity open on to the contested ground of debates over biological and psychological essentialism, the exclusionary politics of feminist theory, and the need to balance feminist demands for equality with a recognition of differences not only between the sexes but also among women who are differently raced and classed. Let me now turn to a second area that is central to the question of gender and objectivity.

QUESTIONING SCIENTIFIC METHOD: SCIENCE AND THE INTERESTS OF KNOWLEDGE

Conventionally, objective knowledge is the goal not just of western philosophy, but of any empirically based science, whether social or physical. It is no accident, as they say, that mathematics provided a model for Descartes. In the interests of universally valid truths, scientists are expected to conduct research and employ methods that are free of error and prejudice. Any contingency that may affect scientific results is ruled out. Scientific projects are considered useful to the extent that the knowledge they produce yields objectively neutral certainties and truths, which are regarded as unbiased and value-free. The processes by which science progresses are generally thought to be empirical, and the knowledge it produces is generally thought to be objective. Subjectivity is eliminated, partiality eradicated, and particularity neutralized. Science is held to be the very paradigm of truth. As Rorty puts it 'Worries about "cognitive status" and "objectivity" are characteristic of a secularized culture in which the scientist replaces the priest' (1994, 35). Thomas Nagel also questions what he refers to as 'scientism':

> Scientism is actually a special form of idealism, for it puts one type of human understanding in charge of the universe and what can be said about it. At its most myopic it assumes that everything there is must be understandable by the employment of scientific theories like those we have developed to date – physics and evolutionary biology are the current paradigms. (1989, 9)

If the diagnoses offered by Nagel and Rorty are similar, their reactions to it differ. Nagel thinks that 'the recognition of our contingency, our finitude, and our containment in the world' should not lead to our 'abandoning the pursuit for truth' or the 'ambition of transcendence, however limited may be our success in achieving it' (Nagel 1989, 9). The image 'that Truth is "out there," up in front of us, waiting for us to reach it' is one that seems to Rorty, as a pragmatist, 'an unfortunate attempt to carry a religious view of the world over into an increasingly secular culture' (1994, 38–9). Rorty wants to 'drop the objective–subjective distinction altogether' and 'to substitute the idea of "unforced agreement" for that of "objectivity"' (1994, 38).

Rorty's views have affinities with Habermas, and follow in the footsteps of Thomas Kuhn, who suggested in *The Structure of Scientific Revolutions* (1962) that scientific theories were not neutral and value-free, thereby casting doubt on the positivist claim that value-judgements are meaningless (Rorty 1994, 38; Code 1993, 17). Feyerabend extends this line of argument in *Against Method* (1975), suggesting that there is no such thing as scientific method, but that 'science itself is a thoroughly irrational discipline' (Bernstein 1983, 4). As Richard Bernstein also points out, Peter Winch (1958), on the other hand, accepts 'the empiricist image of science' (Bernstein 1983, 26) that Feyerabend, Kuhn, and others discredited, in order to emphasize 'the logical gap and the logical incompatibility between natural and social science' and to question Weber's suggestion that statistics are the 'ultimate court of appeal for the validity of sociological interpretations' (27).

In a different vein, we have learned from Foucault, among others, that knowledge reflects the interests of its knowers, and that ostensible truths are informed by power relations. Foucault says that 'the question of ideology that is asked of science is not the question of situations or practices that it reflects more or less consciously; nor is it the question of the possible use or misuse to which it could be put; it is the question of its existence as a discursive practice and of its functioning among other practices' (1972: 185). If science carries with it certain political agendas, if supposedly empirical truths are located within power structures and directed towards the particular ends of certain interest groups, and if the results yielded by science no longer appear to be universally applicable, a number of familiar concepts begin to line themselves up differently. It is no longer clear that objective knowledge can be obtained by disinterested observers through rational methods, or whether this knowledge is subject to the interests of dominant groups with particular interests which interfere with its purported rationality.

Feminists are hardly the first to doubt that science itself may not be as objective and neutral as it takes itself to be. Nor are they alone in challenging the presumption that scientific knowledge will not, as Sandra Harding is fond of putting it, bear the fingerprints of the communities that produce it (see Harding 1991, 83) (1986, 22; 1993, 57). As David Goldberg, editor of *Anatomy of Racism* says: 'Racism is revealed . . . to have taken on in normal course the mantle of scientific theory, philosophical rationality, and "morality." Science, politics, and legality, in turn, are revealed to have addressed themselves more or less explicitly in racial and racist terms' (1990, xiv).

There are several ways of responding to these problems about the partiality of ways of knowing. Here I want to focus, initially, on Sandra Harding's approach.

FEMINIST STANDPOINT THEORY: STRONG OBJECTIVITY

Harding's response is to argue that objectivity is not rigorous enough as a rule; far from abandoning it as an ideal we need to pursue it all the more rigorously:

> The problem with the conventional conception of objectivity is not that it is too rigorous or too 'objectifying,' as some have argued, but that it is *not rigorous or objectifying enough*; it is too weak to accomplish even the goals for which it has been designed, let alone the more difficult projects called for by feminisms and other new social movements. (1993, 50–1)

In order to clarify what is at stake in Harding's call for what she designates 'strong objectivity,' let me situate the claims she made in 1986 alongside a later articulation of how feminists should approach science. Addressing 'all those people inside and outside science who are still wondering just what are the insights about science and knowledge that feminists have to offer,' Harding's goal, as stated in the more recent article, is to highlight the challenge that 'feminist reflections on scientific knowledge' presents to the dominant . . . epistemology and philosophy of science' (1993, 52). In pursuit of this goal, Harding undertakes to rethink the feminist standpoint approach, a position she advocated in *The Science Question in Feminism* (1986), and which she differentiated from two other possible feminist responses to science, namely feminist empiricism and feminist postmodernism.

Feminist intervention in science, as Harding outlines it, has the virtue of enlarging the perspective of science by including 'more women scientists' who 'are more likely than men to notice andro-centric bias' (1986, 25). As such it departs from the traditional notion of science as conducted by researchers whose 'social identity' is assumed to be irrelevant to 'the results of research.' Feminist empiricists argue that women '*as a group* are more likely to produce unbiased and objective results than are men (or non-feminists) as a group' (25). While in one respect feminist empiricism issues a chal-lenge to 'science as usual' – insofar as it no longer assumes that the same results will be achieved irrespective of factors such as gender, class, and race – in another respect it leaves 'unchallenged the exist-ing methodological norms of science' (25). To the extent that this approach maintains that 'sexism and androcentrism are social biases correctable by stricter adherence to the existing methodological norms of scientific inquiry' (24), feminist empiricism identifies only 'bad science as the problem, not science as usual' (25). In other words, feminist empiricists locate the cause of sexist and androcen-tric results in 'insufficient care and rigor in following existing methods and norms (which tend to be empirical)' (1993, 52), and 'call for even greater rigor in using these methods and following these norms' (53).

The advantage of feminist empiricism, which argues that 'the sci-ences have been blind to their own sexist and androcentric research practices and results' is also its weakness in Harding's eyes: 'it explains the production of sexist and nonsexist results of research with only a minimal challenge to the fundamental logic of research' as under-stood by scientists and 'dominant philosophies of science' (53). From the perspective that Harding identifies as the feminist standpoint, a position she articulates by reference to Hegel's master/slave dialectic, this constitutes a failure to adequately address 'the limitations of the dominant conceptions of method and explanation and the ways the conceptions constrain and distort results . . . even when these domi-nant conceptions are most rigorously respected' (53).

From the more radical perspective of feminist standpoint episte-mology that Harding herself endorses, 'men's dominating posi-tion in social life results in partial and perverse understandings, whereas women's subjugated position provides the possibility of more complete and less perverse understandings' (1986, 26). From the feminist standpoint then, as Harding elaborated it in 1986, 'cri-tiques of social and natural science . . . are grounded in the universal features of women's experience as understood from the perspective of feminism' (26). Harding recognizes the problem of positing the universality of women's experience, asking 'Can there be *a* feminist standpoint if women's (or feminists') social experience is divided by class, race, and culture?' and suggesting, with Flax (1986, 17), that 'Perhaps "reality" can have "a" structure only from the falsely universalizing perspective of the master' (Harding [quoting Flax] 1986, 26), and that the feminist standpoint is 'still too firmly rooted in a problematic politics of essentialized identities' (27).

By 1993, Harding had recast standpoint theory so that it 'leads to the refusal to essentialize its subjects of knowledge' (1993, 66). It is noteworthy that this restatement of the feminist standpoint incorporates some of the elements Harding formerly distinguished from her own position, preferring to see them in 1986 as characteristic of a third approach that she labeled 'feminist postmodernism.' This approach embraces 'as a fruitful grounding for inquiry the fractured identities modern life creates' (1986, 28) and demonstrates 'a profound skepticism regarding universal (or universalizing) claims about the existence, nature and powers of reason, progress, science, language and the "subject/self"'' (27–8 [quoting Flax]).

In language reminiscent of the 'fractured identities' which she previously saw as postmodern, Harding speaks of the 'logic of multiple subjects' (1993, 66) that standpoint theory must embrace, emphasizing that 'There is no single, ideal woman's life from which standpoint theories recommend that thought start. Instead, one must turn to all of the lives that are marginalized in different ways by the operative systems of social stratification' (1993, 60). Yet, underlying Harding's position is a tension that is also encountered in Donna Haraway's (1991) position. Neither Harding nor Haraway are willing to give up the search for objectivity or truth. Both embrace the idea that while knowledge is situated, it can also be objective. Haraway is correct to point out that a relativist position is ultimately just as problematic as an ostensibly universalist view from nowhere. Both positions evacuate the significance of situated locatedness. The problem, however, with Haraway is that she wants to reappropriate the language of objectivity in the service of a feminist epistemology, rather than agree that all knowledge is, and will remain, contested. Once we accept that knowledge is interested, that the producers of knowledge are never free of political constraint, then surely the project of feminist theory cannot be merely to redefine objectivity in order to accommodate previously excluded or misconstrued ways of knowing. Rather, the project is to accept that all knowledge is contested, that it should remain contested, and that the conditions under which significant contestations can be aired and debated, in the interests of making publicly available these contested views, need to be preserved. In order to develop alternatives to hegemonic logics and narratives, media space needs to be given to alternative views, and attention needs to be devoted to maintaining a separation between governmental and capitalist interests, and between governmental interests and media legitimacy. Without maintaining the independence of political and intellectual enquiry, by ensuring some degree of autonomy between publishing houses and governmental interests, between media outlets and political representatives of current administrations, there will be few opportunities for informed, political dissent to be heard, or for critical discourse to be generated. The role of educators in this process is absolutely critical. The autonomy of the humanities and social sciences in schools and universities must be maintained.

Received opinion about the status of scientific knowledge has been cast into doubt by philosophers of science and feminists, who find questionable the objectivity of scientific results, and the neutrality of the subject implied by the claims of science to objectivity. Questions have been raised about the legitimacy of disciplines that claim universal knowledge, when those disciplines are still largely populated and promulgated by privileged, white male scientists, who presumably bring to bear their privileged assumptions on their subjects of enquiry. Ideologies that spring uncritically from positions of dominance are now being challenged, in part due to a new group of scientists who are beginning to do science from different perspectives, and in part due to feminist and race theorists whose paradigms of knowledge challenge the drive to universality.

We should note that Harding's conception of strong objectivity has stripped away many of the features that have traditionally been associated with objectivity. Knowledge is no longer construed as universal, ahistorical, or unchanging, observers are not assumed to be neutral or impartial, and the scientist is conceived not simply as an individual seeking truth, but as a member of a group whose interests affect the method and results of scientific projects. The notion of strong objectivity has more in common with what Rorty calls 'unforced agreement' than with conventional ideas of scientific standards. My point here is not to suggest that Rorty's position as a whole is congruent with Harding's, but that the notion of objectivity, as rethought and endorsed by Harding's 'Strong objectivity' thesis, is similar to Rorty's replacement of subject–object dualism by what he calls 'unforced agreement.' Harding differentiates herself from Rorty when she distinguishes her position from ethnocentrism, with which she associates Rorty (1993, 79). It is also worth noting that Harding does not advocate relativism. Rather, standpoint theory

> argues against the idea that all social situations provide equally useful resources for learning about the world and against the idea that they all set equally strong limits on knowledge . . . Standpoint theory provides arguments for the claim that some social situations are scientifically better than others as places from which to start off knowledge projects, and those arguments must be defeated if the charge of relativism is to gain plausibility. (60)

Should we then be seeking, with Harding, a way of 'maximizing objectivity' (57) on the grounds that the conventional conception of objectivity 'is *not rigorous or objectifying enough*' (50–1)? Or are we driven, with Lorriane Code, to a qualified version of relativism? (Code 1993, 40). Perhaps there is a third alternative, which avoids on the one hand appropriating objectivity for feminist ends (à la Harding and Haraway) and on the other hand embracing an insidious relativism. Perhaps we should embrace the view that whatever masquerades under the label of objectivity is in fact necessarily partial, and biased? Is purported knowledge doomed to misrepresent the particular interests of a dominant group as if these interests were unmarked by race, gender, class, neutral, and valid for all, when in fact they merely reflect the usually invisible privilege of those in power? Must we say with Judith Grant that 'reason is gendered' (Grant 1987 [quoted by Hawkesworth 1989, 333])? The problem, in short, is 'how to talk about objectivity in the light of our understanding that all knowledge is socially situated and representation is a political act' (Lennon and Whitford 1994, 5).

Instead of mourning the loss of objectivity, universality, and neutrality, or indulging a nostalgic longing for the disembodied abstract subject of universal rights, perhaps the point is to acknowledge that the standards that were assumed in such a vision were never disinterested: their interests were only occluded. What has passed for knowledge in the western tradition is irrevocably tied to certain beliefs, which might have been invisible precisely because they were deemed irrelevant by those considered legitimate knowers, but which, for all that, did not cease to produce effects upon those excluded from the realm in which knowers exchanged and legitimated what could be known.

If there is good reason to question objectivism with its pretensions to a disembodied, value-free, rational quest for universal truth, there are also serious problems confronting those who want to take on feminist challenges to objectivity. Lennon and Whitford point to one problem when they observe that it is 'difficult to simply abandon objectivity' because 'feminism as a political project requires that the feminist claims of distorting and subordinating trends within masculine knowledge be regarded as legitimate, and legitimate generally, not only for feminists' (1994: 4). Legal theorist Deborah Rhode refers to the same problem under the heading of the 'post-modern paradox' (1991, 333). Those who emphasize the 'social construction of knowledge' have to face the difficulty that this stance 'also limits its own aspirations to authority' since its 'Adherents are left in the awkward position of maintaining that gender oppression exists while challenging our capacity to document it' (333). An example Rhode gives is not incidental to the anecdote I borrowed from Laqueur, and with which I began this chapter. She says 'feminists have a stake both in quantifying the frequency of rape, and in questioning the conventional definitions on which rape statistics are based' (333).

Having established that the space of exclusion constructed by legitimate knowers is worthy of exploration, we must not make the mistake of expecting to tap directly into the experience of those who are other than traditional knowers, as if they were a source of unmediated knowledge that can merely be appropriated, and as if the experience of marginalization does not itself help to construct knowledge. Nor must we adopt an additive model, whereby excluded voices are included in a previously formulated framework, which we envisage along the same lines, but which is simply expanded to incorporate new or alternative visions. This fails to appreciate that what is in question is not just the knowledge itself, where knowledge is understood as a set of cumulative facts about the world; at issue, rather, are the very processes of legitimation by which knowledge comes to acquire the features that validate it as knowledge. If what is counted as knowable is itself dictated by a community of knowers who are also the producers and overseers of the standards that constitute knowledge, then there is a sense in which these knowers must also be credited with designating its others as other. To remain insensitive to this issue is to risk allowing feminism itself to carelessly construct its others, thereby extending the privilege of the dominant group to a few privileged women, at the expense of other women and minority groups. The solution then cannot simply be to turn to these excluded others, on the assumption that their knowledge is somehow purer than that of the dominant group(s). It is not a matter of appealing to a version of false consciousness, or – to return to the source of accounts of false consciousness – it is insufficient to merely reverse the hierarchy so that the Slave gains the upper hand over the Master. The erstwhile slave cannot be assumed to be in an unproblematically privileged relation to the truth any more than the erstwhile master, since what is in question here is the very possibility – and even desirability – of ever attaining a universal standpoint. Narayan warns against the dangers of 'romanticizing' the privilege of marginalized perspectives, suggesting that 'Feminist epistemology . . . must attempt to balance the assertion of the value of a different culture or experience against the dangers of romanticizing it to the extent that the limitations and oppressions it confers on its subjects are ignored' (1989, 257). Haraway makes a similar point when she says, 'There is a premium on establishing the capacity to see from the peripheries and the depths. But here there also lies a serious danger of romanticizing and/or appropriating the vision of the less powerful while claiming to see from their positions' (2003, 395).

Should we aspire to what Thomas Nagel called the 'view from nowhere,' or what Hilary Putnam sees as the 'God's eye view of things,' (1981: 49–50, referred to by Rorty 1994, 24) and Haraway refers to as the 'God-trick' (1991, 189)? Feminists must avoid naïvely privileging the alleged experience of the oppressed, or constructing *the* voice of women, as if the referent of gender were a monolithic, homogeneous group unstratified by multiple identities such as class and race. We must take care not to inadvertently produce our own version of what Lorraine Code calls the ideal that 'through the autonomous exercise of . . . reason' one can 'transcend particularity and contingency' (Code 1993, 16). In an incisive discussion of this problem Martha Minow asks, 'why, when it comes to our own arguments and activities, feminists forget the very insights that animate feminist initiatives, insights about the power of unstated reference points and points of view, the privileged position of the status quo, and the pretense that a particular is the universal?' (1991, 359)

BEYOND FEMINIST EPISTEMOLOGY

Uma Narayan and Patricia Hill Collins, among others, have sought to extend standpoint epistemology so that it can accommodate the perspectives, for example, of third world feminists and African-American feminists. Both Narayan and Collins suggest that it is not enough simply to add perspectives that have been excluded previously, and hope to thereby attain a more complete picture. Narayan says,

> Feminist epistemology suggests that integrating women's contribution into the domain of science and knowledge will not constitute a mere adding of details; it will not merely widen the canvas but result in a shift of perspective enabling us to see a very different picture. The inclusion of women's perspective will not merely amount to women participating in greater numbers in the existing practice of science and knowledge, but it will change the very nature of these activities and their self-understanding. (1989, 256)

Collins makes a similar point: 'Reclaiming the Black feminist intellectual tradition involves much more than developing Black feminist analyses using standard epistemological criteria. It also involves challenging the very definitions of intellectual discourse itself' (1991, 15). If the whole picture has to change, if we need to challenge the very terms of the debate, the project of feminist epistemology cannot be restricted to rewriting history, by writing into it those whose contributions have been heretofore excluded, misrepresented, or denigrated due to gender, race, class, or sexuality. Important though such a task is, we also inherit the delicate problem of formulating a new agenda. How do we avoid constructing a new vision of knowledge that will not fall prey to new normative exclusions to which we remain blind? How does feminist theory become sufficiently inclusive to speak for all women? Is the appropriate response to fine tune feminism so that it is flexible enough that all groups, races, ethnicities, religions, and so on, can be included under the umbrella of feminism, or is it rather a matter of giving up any pretension to universality? Is there a way of drawing provisional conclusions in a manner that renders them open to revision, should new evidence come to light that demands reconsideration of current tenets or beliefs? Rather than attempting absolute and universal solutions, perhaps we need to learn the lesson that we should foster the conditions in which theories are open to continual scrutiny, and subject to revision. This does not mean that we need to be coy about our conclusions, rather that we need to admit that we are willing to revise them should informed critique convince us that they are wrong. Above all we should be working to maintain a democratic society in which such critiques can be heard and can be influential. Rather than trying to rule out agonistic politics, Chantal Mouffe (1993) has called for a democracy in which the conditions for dissent and debate are maintained – a call that seems increasingly urgent in an age in which the ownership of media outlets is concentrated in the hands of a few corporations, in which the line between corporate and political interests is becoming increasingly difficult to discern, and in which reluctance to criticize and expose government incompetence, corruption, and misrepresentation is widespread. Critical debate depends upon the dissemination of accurate information – which has been largely lacking in mainstream media outlets since the lead up to the Iraq war. Those who manipulated and withheld information have not been held accountable. Or rather, they have been allowed to determine what constitute standards of 'accuracy'.

CHAPTER 5

POSTCOLONIAL FEMINIST THEORY: THE RHETORICAL CLASH OF 'EAST' AND 'WEST'

The object of postcolonial feminist theory is not a simple one. Not only are feminists working in postcolonial contexts often beset with the responsibility, in some shape or other, to shoulder the burden of competing versions of nationalism; history also runs interference with any simple divide between the colonial and the postcolonial. Take the complicated positionality of a third world feminist who situates herself in relation to India, for example. To identify oneself as South Asian in order to avoid the hegemonic overtones of nationalism is not merely to align oneself with Bangladesh, Bhutan, India, Nepal, Pakistan, and Sri Lanka. As Bhattacharjee (1997) cautions, even the term South Asian can be problematic when used to designate an Indian woman, since – given its history – India itself is in some respects imperialist in relation to its neighbors, Pakistan and Bangladesh. Or, in another context, writing just before Britain ceded its colonial rule of Hong Kong to China, Rey Chow says 'the idea that China, simply because it is a communist, "third world" nation, should be exempt from the charges of colonialism, imperialism, and racism is impossible' (1998, xxi). Similarly, pointing to Stefan Tanaka's work, *Japan's Orient*, Chow points out that 'a non-Western culture, Japan, also produces its own "orient"' (1998, 190 n. 13). Chow goes on to say that we need to move 'beyond the East–West dichotomy of Edward Said's *Orientalism* by showing Orientalism to be an "Eastern" as well as "Western" historical phenomenon' (1998, 191 n. 13).

In an attempt both to rebut those who seek to dismiss, trivialize, or undermine the claims of third world women to feminism, and to expose and render unstable the mythical constructions of 'East' and 'West' embraced by Indian postcolonial nationalism on the one hand and the version of nationalism espoused in the wake of British colonial rule in India on the other, Uma Narayan problematizes the need to situate herself as a 'third world feminist' (1997).While mainstream feminists can assume that the position from which they speak is understood, third world feminists are compelled by the hegemony of feminist theory to locate themselves, to render an account of their specific situation, before they can begin to speak or be heard. Narayan confronts an implicit demand to render accessible the place from which she speaks, to confess her origins as deviant or marginal, to explain herself, a demand that those who assume the privilege of dictating the terms of the debate do not face. Such a demand issues from several different directions. Mainstream, western, feminist theory requires her to situate her identity as non-white. Those who are in the process of articulating and defending a postcolonial nationalist platform demand from her a justification of her turn to feminist theory. Narayan points out how women get caught in the middle of the competing narratives provided by colonial powers and the colonized parties, so that any feminist criticism is seen as a betrayal of their culture, as if feminists are selling out to western colonial visions. Even members of her own family, including her mother, require an explanation of her feminism.

Narayan shows that, in fact, far from being imported to India as an ostensibly enlightened western idea, her feminist practice is indebted to the struggles that she confronted within her own family. She watched her mother struggle with her mother-in-law, in a joint family, which was still patriarchal in many ways. She discusses how her feminist consciousness was forged precisely because of the fact that she witnessed the silencing of her mother, and points to the irony that her mother is critical of her feminism, as if it were due to the corrupting influence of the west. Narayan thus draws out the contradictory messages to which she was exposed. On the one hand, her mother wanted to do her duty in bringing up her daughter well, but on the other hand she encouraged her daughter to get an education – yet the very ideas to which this education exposed Narayan were suspect in her mother's eyes. Asked to uphold traditional nationalist values, Narayan shows how her mother was invested in the expectation that her daughter safeguard the very culture that Narayan witnessed as oppressing her mother.

The contradictory messages to which Narayan was exposed in her relationship with her mother function as a metaphor for the idealization and totalization at work in the ways that both the east and the west represent themselves. Thus, for example, traditional Indian nationalists constructed sati, the practice of widow immolation, as if it were emblematic of 'Indian culture.' That is, the religiously and ethnically variegated cultures of India are represented as a homogeneous and monolithic other of an equally imaginary and oversimplified conception of the west. Narayan observes that not only the 'west' but also Indian nationalists evoke a picture of the pristine, spiritual tradition, in which women knew their place, by constructing sati as a much more widespread practice than in fact it is.

By weaving together an autobiographical account with theoretical analyses, Narayan is able to answer that demand to be answerable, as a third world feminist, to a politics of location, even as she problematizes it. She argues that women's bodies often become the casualties of selective versions of nationalism, in this case the ground on which idealized and totalizing conceptions of the 'East' and 'West' compete with one another. Expected to safeguard the purity of nationalist myths, women are made to represent the 'tradition' and 'spirituality' to which fundamentalist Indian nationalists turn, in an atavistic maneuver that appeals to a mythical, prehistorical, 'essence' of India, which is itself constructed in reaction to the imposition of British colonization. The colonial western world persists in representing itself as enshrining the values of liberty and equality, in order to oppose what were consequently perceived as barbaric eastern practices, while in fact perpetrating the barbarism of slavery and colonialism. The western world continues to cast itself in the role of liberator of the free world, to claim the high moral ground of innocence and justice, while in fact operating according to the demands of capitalism, and committing itself to continued abuses of freedom.

This appeal to the rhetoric of freedom and equality by colonial empires conveniently forgets (or sublimates?) its colonial exploitation and support of the slave trade, while castigating India for what it represents as primitive practices. Sati is trundled out as emblematic of the whole of India, in a move that forgets that Hinduism is not the only religion in India, and overlooks the fact that the practice was relatively isolated both historically and geographically. It is a case of 'white men . . . saving brown women from brown men,' as Spivak famously put it (1988, 296). Or, as Ramla Khalidi and Judith Tucker observe in the context of the Middle East:

In the nineteenth century and the first half of the twentieth century, colonial powers repeatedly used the issue of gender to advance their own agendas in the region. They argued that the oppression of women justified colonial intervention, and that the imperial project would elevate women to the standard of equality putatively present in northern Europe. The debatable sincerity and validity of these claims aside, the linking of gender issues to Western intervention and the invocation of Western standards to which all must aspire left a bitter legacy of mistrust. (1996, 9)

The conflict between anti-colonial nationalism and 'westernization' in third world contexts should be understood by way of the strategic – or what Narayan calls the 'rhetorical' (1997, 29) – use of the term 'westernization.' When anti-colonial nationalists repudiate feminism on the grounds that it is merely another version of western colonial influence, they do so by defining western values in a way that suits their needs. As Narayan says, 'in Third World contexts ... there is an *extremely selective* rejection of "Westernization"' (1997, 22). That is, Hindu fundamentalists see no contradiction in castigating western values on the one hand, and 'skillfully us[ing] contemporary media such as television to propagate their ideological messages' (1997, 22), on the other.

I suggest that a similar dynamic is at play in Deepa Mehta's film *Fire*, to which I now turn. Narayan's argument provides a useful framework for considering a film that also explores the clash between 'East' and 'West,' at the same time as it problematizes, as Namita Goswami (whose help has been invaluable in writing this chapter) puts it, 'East' and 'East' (2006). Both Narayan and Mehta are concerned with the way in which women are positioned as the ground on which such conflicts get played out, and the need to re-imagine the possibilities of subjectivity and community.

Jatin (Jaaved Jaaferi) has married Sita (Nandita Das) in an arranged marriage, the audience learns, as they watch the newly married couple tour the Taj Mahal, symbol of eternal love. On the one hand, Jatin has capitulated to the pressure exerted by his brother, Ashok (Kulbushan Kharbanda), and mother, Biji (Kushal Rekhi), that he should get married – an expectation that is all the more pressing because Ashok and Radha (Shabana Azmi) are unable to have children, so that the continuation of the family name is up to Jatin. On the other hand, he refuses to give up his Chinese girlfriend Julie (Alice Poon), with whom he is still in love. Julie refuses to marry him because she wants to maintain the excitement of their attraction to one another – the hunt, as she calls it, a game in which the object, as she sees it, is to remain prey to capture, not to get caught in the snare of marriage.

Jatin wants his wife, Sita, to wear mini-skirts, but he also suggests that she has a baby, which would keep her 'occupied.' While he understands why Julie, his westernized girlfriend, does not want to become a 'baby-making machine,' he seems to have little trouble imposing this expectation on Sita. His appeal to both 'eastern' and 'western' traditions is highly selective, allowing him to fail to see the contradiction between expecting Sita to conform to his ideal of what a traditional Indian woman is supposed to be, while at the same time judging her as falling short of the western influences that Julie embodies. He benefits from the cooking that Sita and Radha do in order to sustain the take-out store, while he rents pornography to children on the side. Radha's husband, Ashok, for his part, devotes himself to his religious Swami, sublimating his sexual desire in religion. He has renounced his sexual desire, believing that 'desire is the root of all evil,' that 'desire brings ruin.'

The question that the film asks is, to what does desire bring ruin? Is it to the tradition that so binds Sita and Radha to their husbands as dutiful wives, and which makes Sita, in her words, react like a 'trained monkey' when the right buttons are pushed? Is it to the religious sensibility to which Ashok aspires, and to which Sita and Radha adhere as they fast in loyalty and devotion to their husbands? Is it to the stability of a household that maintains an outer façade of respectability, as Radha's mute and dependent mother-in-law, Biji, sits silently presiding over it, ringing a hand bell when she needs something, but helpless to verbalize her protest as she observes the breaking of sexual taboos to which she is involuntary witness?

Biji's stroke has rendered her speechless and immobile. Symbolically, her fading matriarchal power is thus established. She sees everything that goes on, and while she doesn't speak, she rings her bell in order to signal disapproval. As the mother of Jatin and Ashok, she lives with them in a joint family, much like the one Narayan describes, in which Radha and Sita in their role as wives are expected to wash, dress, and feed her. Biji shows her disgust at the relationship that springs up between Radha and Sita by spitting in Radha's face (in this case, ringing the bell does not suffice!), in a moment that abjects Radha, as well as Sita. This gesture of bodily expulsion is ironically apt, given that Radha has devoted herself to tending to Biji's bodily and personal needs, bathing, powdering, and feeding her, maintaining her body as clean and proper. If the abjection of this moment underlines Biji's helplessness, as she musters all her energy to express her disgust by spitting mucous at her daughter-in-law – thereby externalizing what should remain inside, commenting on the fate that she thinks should have met Radha's and Sita's sexual feelings for one another – it also aligns Biji with her son, and pits her against the women who have transgressed the patriarchal order. The film suggests Biji's reaction is prompted by the threat their relationship presents not only to Ashok but also to the heterosexual and patriarchal order that girds the symbolic order that is 'India.'

Ashok has taken a vow of celibacy. For thirteen years, after learning that his wife Radha cannot bear children, he has not touched her, in order to put himself beyond temptation and closer to God. He still requires Radha to lie next to him, to make certain that he is beyond temptation. It is Radha's duty, as his wife, he tells her, to help him. Juxtaposed to this perversion of desire is Mundu (Ranjit Chowdhry), the household servant, who makes it his habit to watch pornographic videos in the company of Biji, whom he is supposed to look after. Radha walks in on him one day and when she scolds him he retaliates by telling Ashok, Radha's husband, about the 'hanky panky' that he has observed between Radha and Sita in their husbands' absence. While Ashok's life is taken up with religious aspirations, and Jatin is preoccupied with running a pornographic video business on the side, and seeing his girlfriend Julie whenever he can, Mundu decrees that Radha and Sita are sullying the family name. That it is a servant who is most interested, at least ostensibly, in defending the respectability of the family name, presents an irony that subsists in his precarious social status, as both subservient to the family and invested in its stability.

Confronted with the sight of his wife's desire as it is expressed in her relationship with Sita, all the boundaries change for Ashok. In another moment of abjection, in which he forces himself on his wife, several forces converge. Ashok overcomes thirteen years of self-denial in order to keep at bay a desire that is foreign to his own, in order to attempt to re-establish a semblance of the proper order. But it can only be a semblance, since his religious fanaticism has put into question what constitutes the proper order of relations between himself and his wife: he has lived his life at the expense of hers, excluding any recognition of her as a desiring subject. He has asked her to find meaning in being a dutiful wife, in answering only to his desire, a desire which has been directed towards religious transcendence. Ashok must build again, from the foundation up, a system of meaning, as a way of coming to terms with the intolerable: not only does his wife have a desire of her own, but it has an object other than him, an object other than that which the heterosexual order designates. This is something that he cannot take on within his current system of references, which excludes the possibility of her being a subject, of her being a desiring being, of her having an object of desire. The meaning of his world collapses. If his own desire is aroused by the sight of his wife with another woman, he must find a way to exclude that provocation, even at the risk of repudiating his religious aspirations. He must regain control of the clean and proper, and in doing so, he must assert his will over Radha, impose his desire on her, eradicate and eliminate any possibility that her desire could be misdirected. Concentrated in the physical force with which he takes back what he sees as rightfully his – a right he has voluntarily forfeited for thirteen years – is the need to exclude what he has seen and felt, which is intolerable and unacceptable to him. It is so much beyond the pale that it demands that he fire Mundu, witness to his shame. If he abjects Radha, as he takes hold of her, kisses her, and embraces her, he also abjects himself. For in this moment he succumbs to the torrent of desire that he has held back, with Radha's help, for thirteen years, by giving bodily expression to the desire summoned by the memory of Sita and Radha's sexual enjoyment of one another. He gives in to what he has tried so hard to keep at bay, to exclude, to refuse, to control. The trigger for his bodily assertion of his matrimonial right is the inadmissible challenge that Sita's desire for Radha and Radha's desire for Sita presents to him and his belief system. Their abjection as spurned wives is an abjection that is sanctified by that system. Their response to that abjection – to find solace in one another – is not tolerated by the system. And so, in Ashok's eyes, the system – one in which he can repudiate his wife in favor of religious asceticism – must change.

Bringing to mind Narayan's argument, the women in *Fire* are caught in the middle of competing, imaginary, totalizing, and idealized visions. They are required to play the role of 'second-class' citizens in the competing visions of 'East' and 'West.' Sita and Radha are expected to remain in their subordinate positions, to represent the purity of traditional Hindu culture, while their husbands direct their erotic energies elsewhere. Hence Mehta's nod to the trial by fire in Hindu mythology that Sita undergoes. The theme of sati hovers in the background of the film, as the idea of goddess Sita's purity, and her trial by fire is repeatedly revisited, for example when Radha's sari catches fire in the kitchen, after Ashok pushes her away in disgust at her lack of response. As Rahul Gairola says:

> Perhaps it is no surprise that Mehta names her two heroines after two Hindu goddesses in the same way that widow-burning bestows upon the acquiescent widow the identity of Sati. Unlike the subaltern women of Spivak's essay, Mehta's heroines forge new models of representation in our tele-visual age that offer cathartic options to patriarchal life in India. (2002, 322)

By evoking the trial by fire, but transforming its meaning, so that Radha emerges unscathed by the fire and is able to join Sita (at a Muslim shrine – the symbolism of which does not go unnoticed), Mehta rewrites Hindu mythology. As Leela Gandhi puts it, Spivak argues that 'the "gendered subaltern" disappears because we never hear her speak about herself,' because 'she is simply the medium through which competing discourses represent their claims' (1998, 90). We should be wary of embracing Mehta's heroines, Sita and Radha, then, as if they represented an uncomplicated revolutionary impulse. Quoting Stuart Hall, Tania Murray Li reminds us that 'subaltern subjectivities are formed within hegemonic relations' and that 'the process of ideological struggle seldom involves a "whole new alternative set of terms" but proceeds rather through the attempt to "win some new set of meanings through an existing term or category . . . dis-articulating it from its place in the signifying structure" and "rearticulating its associations" with other ideas and with particular social forces' (2003, 385). To put a slightly different spin on this, we should be cautious of critiques of the film that dismiss the lesbian relationship because it is only out of despair of their unsatisfactory marital relationships that Sita and Radha turn to one another. In the context of taking seriously the contradictions that situate third world women, which Narayan allows us to explore, *Fire* can be read as resignifying reactive, masculinist, postcolonial nationalist narratives, by opening up new ways of imagining female desire.

In the press release for Zeitgeist Films Mehta says she

> wanted to make a film about contemporary, middle-class India, with all its vulnerabilities, foibles, and the incredible, extremely dramatic battle that is waged daily between the forces of tradition and the desire for an independent, individual voice . . . The struggle between tradition and individual expression is one that takes place in every culture . . . My mother's arranged marriage and her feelings of isolation moved me deeply . . . We women, especially Indian women, constantly have to go through a metaphorical test of purity in order to be validated as human beings, not unlike Sita's trial by fire. (Mehta at Zeitgeistfilms.com)

The reception of the film in India illustrated many of the tensions Mehta attempted to bring to light, prompting a predictable outcry among those who cast themselves as trying to defend an overly schematic version of Indian tradition, understood to embody a morality that was being threatened by Mehta.

Fire opens with a shot of a meadow strewn with a sea of long grass and wild, yellow flowers, among which a mother, a father, and a girl are sitting. A voiceover tells us that a long time ago there were people living in the mountains who had never seen the sea. The mother tells the young girl, an earlier incarnation of Radha, that to see the ocean you just have to 'see without looking,' an image that governs the film, as the relationship between Radha, now a married woman, and Sita, her newly wed sister-in-law, unfolds. By the end of the film, in a flashback to her as a little girl, which also functions as a portent for female desire, symbolized by the ocean, Radha declares, 'I can see the ocean. I can see it.' She has learned the lesson her mother had tried to teach her. Learning to see things differently can be at the same time enormously difficult and ridiculously easy. Sometimes, Mehta seems to be saying, we try so hard, that our efforts get in our way.

No discussion of postcolonial feminist theory would be complete without some consideration of the influential and important input of Spivak, whose work has been cited only intermittently so far. Spivak exploded onto the scene of what has come to be known in England and America as 'continental philosophy' – consisting largely of French and German twentieth-century philosophy – in 1976 with the publication of her translation of Derrida's *De la grammatologie* (1967). The translation, *Of Grammatology*, was accompanied by a long introduction, also by Spivak, which continues to be an invaluable resource for anyone interested in the work of Derrida. It was not until later that Spivak began her interventions into postcolonial theory – for which she has become even more renowned – producing work which bears the traces of the abiding influence of Derrida.

To Spivak's considerable credit, she avoids any easy resolution of her 'position' in terms of deciding either in favor of Derrida or against him. She continues to allow his philosophical corpus to inform her work, certainly championing him over Deleuze and Foucault, while at the same time pointing out the 'specific absence' of 'the imperialist constitution of the colonial subject' (1988, 294) from his work. Spivak is appreciative of Derrida's relentless refusal to take his own position for granted: never one to claim an uncomplicated relationship to any ground of purity, originality, or innocence, Derrida's work is known for highlighting issues of contamination, double logics, and supplementarity. Above all, Spivak is sensitive to the thematics according to which Derrida distances himself from assuming that he could ever occupy a self-transparent stance, as if he were immune from his own implication in the very systems of thought of which he is critical. I shall follow Spivak's own scrupulous practice in this regard, in refusing to ascribe any rigid line of demarcation to separate that which constitutes 'continental philosophy' from that which constitutes 'postcolonial feminist theory' – a distinction that the mainstreaming of Spivak's own theoretical corpus should help to throw into disarray. I do so in full acknowledgement of the dangers to which I open myself: might I not be accused of recuperating the discourse of the subaltern, taming it in the name of 'French feminism' (insofar as the latter is considered the illegitimate sister of 'continental philosophy')? It is a risk I am prepared to take, since the parallels I will draw are limited, strategic, and, as far as possible, drawn from a vigilance not only to the problematics Derrida and Kristeva have explored, but also those to which Spivak alerts us.

Born in 1942, a few years before India won its independence from British colonial rule, Spivak studied in Calcutta, and subsequently at Cornell University, in Ithaca, New York, and at Cambridge, England. In one of her most influential essays, 'French Feminism in an International Frame,' Spivak describes her decision to pursue the study of English as 'highly overdetermined' (1987, 134). The inclusion of the Irish poet Yeats, on whom Spivak focused in her early academic career, under the rubric of 'English' literature bespeaks its own tale of cultural, political, and economic hegemony. One might describe Spivak's interest in Derrida as also heavily overdetermined, this time by those with whom she came into contact in her postgraduate years in the US, in what Spivak has described as 'the most opulent university system in the world' (Harasym 1990, 142). In the 70s and 80s, Derrida was to become virtually obligatory for every English graduate student to master, particularly in the US. One culls a sense of how much Derrida was in the air from, among many other texts, Spivak's 'Finding Feminist Readings: Dante-Yeats' (1987, 15–29). It is the influence of Derrida's 'critique of phallogocentrism' (1987, 134), along with Irigaray's essay on Freud in *Speculum*, to which Spivak credits her initial engagement with feminism, although she will later distance herself from Irigaray's (1985) overly European identification and philosophy.

In another highly influential essay, 'Can the Subaltern Speak?' – an essay which Spivak describes as the 'second step' (Landry and Maclean 1996, 288) to 'French feminism in an International Frame' – Spivak builds on the work of Antonio Gramsci (1971) and that of Ranajit Guha (see Guha and Spivak 1988) to develop a meditation on the subaltern. In what came to be a controversial claim, Spivak begins the final paragraph of the essay with the words 'The subaltern cannot speak' (1988, 308). Donna Landry and Gerald Maclean explain the subaltern as 'that constituency which remains most excluded from the circuits and possible benefits of socialized capital.' To claim 'that the subaltern "cannot speak"' means that:

> the subaltern as such cannot be heard by the privileged of either the First or Third Worlds. If the subaltern were able to make herself heard – as has happened when particular subalterns have emerged, in Antonio Gramsci's terms, as organic intellectuals and spokespeople for their communities – her status as a subaltern would be changed utterly; she would cease to be subaltern. And that is the goal of the ethical relation Spivak is seeking and calling for – that the subaltern, the most oppressed and invisible constituencies, as such might cease to exist. (1996, 5–6)

While Landry and Maclean provide a useful point of entry, it is perhaps still more informative to track Spivak's own responses to,

and rewriting of, the trope of the subaltern. Since the populariza-
tion of the essay 'Can the Subaltern Speak?' first published in 1988
(although an earlier essay appears in 1985 under the title 'Can the
Subaltern Speak? Speculations on widow sacrifice'), Spivak has
responded to critics of the essay, warning of the danger of cavalier
appropriations of the term for use in a first world context (see
Harasym 1990, 142–3). In a 1993 interview Spivak says:

> the word 'subaltern' is losing its definitive power because it has
> become a kind of buzzword for any group that wants something
> that it does not have. People no longer say 'Third World' easily:
> they know that every time they say 'Third World' they have to say
> 'the so-called Third World.' There has been a very strong critical
> debate about whether 'postcolonial' is okay anymore. So 'subal-
> tern' has somehow come to stand for all of that. (Landry and
> Maclean 1996, 290)

Spivak emphasizes the necessary impurity of the subaltern, pointing out that in explicating an alternative version of history to that
provided either by British historians or by Indian nationalists, Guha
and others have focused attention on the chain of peasant uprisings
that have tended to turn into something else:

> every moment of insurgency that [the Subalternists] have fastened
> onto has been a moment when subalternity has been brought to a
> point of crisis: the cultural constructions that are allowed to exist
> within subalternity, removed as it is from other lines of mobility,
> are changed into militancy. In other words, every moment that
> is noticed as a case of subalternity is undermined. We are never
> looking at the pure subaltern. There is, then, something of a not-
> speakingness in the very notion of subalternity. (Landry and
> Maclean 1996, 289)

This impurity of the subaltern is worth pausing over.
    Despite the justified critique of Kristeva's romanticization of
Chinese women that Spivak includes in 'Can the Subaltern Speak?'
there is another moment in Kristeva that communicates with
Spivak's concerns about the impossibility of understanding the subaltern in its purity. In *Powers of Horror* (1982) Kristeva explores the
themes of abjection, sacrifice, and impurity in ways that are deeply

resonant with Derrida's considerations of the constitutive outside, the necessity of being contaminated by, or implicated in, the very target of one's critique, and the *pharmakon* (see Derrida 1981a) as both poison and cure. Bringing together insights as theoretically divergent as Melanie Klein's (1986) psychoanalytic notion of projective identification and Mary Douglas's (1999) anthropological explorations into cultural taboos and ways of ordering and discriminating the pure from the impure, or the disgusting from the decent or palatable, Kristeva's concerns in *Powers of Horror* might very easily be mapped on to Spivak's investigations in 'Can the Subaltern Speak?' It is worth noting that Spivak also finds inspiration in the work of Klein (see for example Landry and Maclean 1996, 398–400). In 'Can the Subaltern Speak?' Spivak points out that in outlawing sati, 'the British in India collaborated and consulted with learned Brahmans' only to efface 'the history of the long period of collaboration' in the final writing of the law, pitting the 'noble Hindu' against the 'bad Hindu' (1988, 301). The logic according to which Hindus are segregated depending on whether they agree or not with the conclusions reached by British imperialists, reflects an attempt to disentangle the pure from the impure, as if one were incommensurable with, and unrelated to, the other. So too does the logic of abjection surface in the judgement finally passed by the British on sati. Quoting Pandurang Vaman Kane's *History of the Dharmasastra*, Spivak points out that sati was judged to be 'revolting' by the British. It was, one might say, condemned as a sickening, barbaric practice of a primitive people, one capable of eliciting physical revulsion, a disgusting act that only served to justify the intervention of British imperialists, who could use its denigration in order to adopt the high ground of moral innocence, in order to condemn those who were clearly ethically incapable of governing themselves. The barbarism of colonialism is thereby conveniently excused – or, one might say, projected, on to those who become targets of white, western 'morality.' Denying the atrocities of their own acts, the British had no trouble in making 'bad Hindus' the repositories of all that is bad, having them stand for what could not be acknowledged – according to the double standard of savior/primitive established by colonialism – in themselves. This, then, is the moment at which I would see not so much a correspondence as what Deleuze might consider a passing between, a becoming other, whereby the two different concepts of Kristeva and Spivak inhabit different 'planes of immanence.' The concepts of purity and impurity operate differently in postcolonial feminist theory and psychoanalytic feminist theory. They are respectively composed by different components, and their plateaus or terrains diverge.

One can trace Spivak's preoccupation with the theme that will come to be known under the heading of the subaltern back to one of the strains running through 'French Feminism in an International Frame' (1987; originally published in 1981). If in this essay Spivak provides a trenchant critique of what might be called Kristeva's orientalism in her book *About Chinese Women* (1977), at the same time, she raises a series of questions about her own positionality vis-à-vis the 'millions of illiterate rural and urban Indian women who live "in the pores of" capitalism, inaccessible to the capitalist dynamics that allow us our shared channels of communication, the definition of common enemies' (1987, 135). Spivak does not fail to bring into question the assumption of privilege that informs her use of the word 'us.' Who is this we? In whose name does Spivak speak? One might say that she speaks as a 'female academic' (134), as part of a group of 'women who, by comparison with the world's women at large, are already infinitely privileged' (150). As Derrida asks in the final line of his essay, 'The Ends of Man,' on which Spivak draws, 'Mais qui, nous?' 'But who, we?' (1982, 136; 1972, 164). Who, then, is this 'we' in whose name Spivak speaks as a female academic? Spivak problematizes the privilege she can assume as a female academic, educated in colonial India, and in the 'West' – in England and in America. She problematizes it by examining the stance that Kristeva (a displaced Bulgarian, and a French intellectual) takes towards Chinese women, and by taking her distance from such privilege. She problematizes it by interrogating her own intellectual trajectory, and by pointing out the need to trouble the category of the 'female academic,' a label that operates as if the only salient characteristic to be marked is that women are not men. What about the privilege of western, white, middle-class women that such a label fails to mark? Spivak puts into question not only her own ideological relationship to 'French feminism,' overdetermined as it is by her Anglo-European education, but also her class privilege in relation to those who have not learned the languages and idioms of culturally, politically, and economically dominant elites – the people, the workers, the peasants, the subaltern, or – to use the example to which Spivak herself refers – an illiterate Indian woman. Spivak refuses to assume her own superiority to such groups, seeking to avoid on the one hand a patronizing attitude toward them, and on the other an overly nostalgic celebration of them, as if they represented 'the especial beauty of the old' (1987, 135). She asks instead, what it would mean to 'learn from and speak to' them (135).

In 'French Feminism in an International Frame' Spivak constructs her discussion around the problematics of clitoridectomy and around the continued ideological proprietorship British imperialism exerts over India, even after technically granting India its independence in 1947. If an 'ancient washerwomen . . . washing clothes in the river,' whose claim to a part of a river is contested by another, is, strictly speaking, wrong in her assertion in 1949 that the river belongs to the East India Company, ideologically she is right: the river still belongs to the British for all intents and purposes. The washerwoman, then, is both right and wrong at the same time: empirically speaking she is incorrect, but ideologically speaking she is right – the river and those who wash clothes in it are owned by, overdetermined by, or belong to the legacy of British colonialism in incalculable and labyrinthine ways. Their horizons, their discourse, their lives, their practices, their possibilities are not suddenly rendered different by the fact that Britain sees fit to finally sign over to India the land it had appropriated in 1858. Certain individuals will indeed develop a discourse about how to construe a postcolonial, nationalist, Indian identity, and some intellectuals will insist that such a postcolonial version of nationalism should not be restricted to an oppositional politics – one that merely adopts a reactive stance to British imperialism, shaping itself in an attempt to incarnate everything that the legacy of British rule and custom is not. Yet you can rest assured that the views of two elderly washerwomen are unlikely to have much impact on the niceties of how to formulate a viable postcolonial Indian nationalism.

Targeting Deleuze and Foucault (1977), in 'Can the Subaltern Speak?' (1988) for failing to take seriously the international division of labor as implicated in the exploitation of a third world underclass (with all the caveats such a descriptor requires), Spivak also takes aim at them for painting a picture of the ideal revolutionary in terms of the European working class, the experience of which constitutes, by default, 'reality' or 'truth,' as if occupying an incontestable position of authenticity which it is the intellectual's job to merely report. Against this context, Spivak is interested in avoiding the assumption that the working class has direct access to universal truths, reminding us of the awkward problem of ideology, at the same time as insisting that the intellectual's view of things is predicated on economic privilege. So, the working class does not hold views that intellectuals can unproblematically tap into, as if such views encapsulated, writ large, the truth. At the same time as remaining critical of the assumption that the workers represent 'reality' – as if their unmediated experience constituted some pre-existing pure kernel of truth, posited as outside theory, and yet somehow available to be accessed and communicated by those who are, as it were, in the know, Spivak wants to grapple with the difficult problem of authority, hegemony, and representation. Who is entitled to speak for whom, and who is to say that they get it right? As soon as you translate the experience of the oppressed into some ostensibly theoretically illuminating proposition, isn't there a sense in which you have already vacated the alleged authenticity of the voice of the people, and transformed it into something else – something more arcane, esoteric, and abstract? Championing a version of Marx and Derrida over Foucault and Deleuze, Spivak utilizes Gramsci's notion of the subaltern, also taken up by Ranajit Guha, in order to pursue these issues.

Whether it is a matter of Derrida's critique of the metaphysics of presence, or feminism's critique of patriarchy, Spivak is at pains to point out the necessity of thinking through one's own 'complicity' (1988, 293) with the very structures from which one seeks some distance. Focusing on the issue of transparency, Spivak points to Derrida's 'awareness of the itinerary of the discourse of presence in [his] *own* critique, a vigilance precisely against too great a claim for transparency' (1988, 293). Similarly, a feminism that proceeds by ignoring the question of the subaltern woman is implicated in 'an unacknowledged political gesture that has a long history and collaborates with a masculine radicalism that renders the place of the investigator transparent' (1988, 295). To act as if the subaltern woman is of no concern to feminism is to claim a space for feminism that is innocent of postcolonial oppression, a space that is uncontaminated by a racist, imperialist history of exploitation. As a thinker who remains vigilant about the impossibility of ever standing definitively outside such privileged narratives – be they the official histories of metaphysics or those of mainstream feminism – Derrida, and his itinerary, remains fertile and instructive for Spivak. This is precisely because 'as a European philosopher he articulates the *European* Subject's tendency to constitute the Other as marginal to ethnocentrism' (1988, 293). Likewise, Spivak resolutely refuses to assume a position of innocence. This does not mean that she is beyond calling out certain intellectuals whose own collusion with the alleged transparency of the positions they assume she sees as exemplary of a systematic cover up of 'sanctioned ignorance' (1988, 291). It means, rather, that Spivak is willing to extend her suspicion of the purity of intentions to herself, reminding us that 'it is important to acknowledge our complicity in the muting [of subalterns by the liberal multiculturalist metropolitan academy], in order precisely to be more effective in the long run. Our work cannot succeed if we always have a scapegoat' (1999, 309).

Those of us who occupy positions which can only be assumed thanks to our insertion into systems of privilege – however such insertion might have been earned – are liable to be targeted as symptomatic of that privilege. In 'Can the Subaltern Speak?' Foucault and Deleuze become the fall guys, having been afforded the privilege and the right to learning, and having abused their position as prominent 'imperialist' subjects and intellectuals, in assuming that their recognition as authoritative scholars, and their consequent right to be heard, is not predicated on the specific silencing of others. Spivak articulates the subtext of that silencing by pointing out that the 'subaltern woman will be as mute as ever' (1988, 295), even as her silencing facilitates not just the rights of others to be heard, but informs the very meanings that attach to their speech. 'Deleuze and Foucault,' says Spivak, 'ignore both the epistemic violence of imperialism and the international division of labor' (1988, 289). Spivak marks out the debts owed to those other others – the poorly remunerated productivity of (often female) workers in labor intensive multinational industries, located with easy access to third world slums, directly supports the comparatively luxurious existence of first world intellectuals. Yet their existence is not thematized in the texts of European philosophy. Their non-thematization makes possible everything that is said there – the other has always already been assimilated, eaten up, accounted for in advance, before ever having been heard, listened to, or understood. In this sense, Spivak gives voice to the washerwoman who knows, in some sense that goes beyond the empirical facts, and flies in the face of reason, that the river in which she washes her clothes still belongs to the East India

Company, that her horizons are severely circumscribed by the implacable history of colonialism.

If in 'French Feminism in an International Frame' it is a conversation between two women washing clothes in a river that provides the narrative and political context for Spivak's reflections, in 'Can the Subaltern Speak?' Spivak develops her enquiry by taking up the problematic of sati, as her reference point, an account to which she returns in *A Critique of Postcolonial Reason* (1999), when she revisits the essay 'Can the Subaltern Speak?' In 1926 Bhubaneswari Bhaduri killed herself while menstruating. Spivak reads her suicide, to which she was impelled because she was unable to carry through the task of 'political assassination' entrusted to her by a group involved in the 'armed struggle for independence' (1988, 307), against the background of sati, a practice in which a 'Hindu widow ascends the pyre of the dead husband and immolates herself upon it' (1988, 297). True to her commitment to thinking through questions of complicity and her acknowledgement of the impossibility of maintaining a genuinely transparent stance, Spivak distances herself, in her understanding of sati, both from the British imperialist condemnation of it, and from what she calls 'Indian nativist' (1988, 297) arguments. If the British imperialist stance is 'a case of "White men saving brown women from brown men,"' the Indian nativist argument is 'a parody of the nostalgia for lost origins: "The women actually wanted to die"' (1988, 297).

If the motives of the condemnation of sati by British imperialists need to be complicated by reading them in terms of diversionary tactics – as a deflection of morally bankrupt colonial practices – so too does the position of those who locate a woman's 'freewill in self-immolation,' the 'profound irony' (1988, 303) of which does not escape Spivak. Nor does the fact that the injunction to a wife to burn herself on her husband's death is conceived in terms of a 'release' from the 'female body' fail to register as presupposing 'the peculiar misfortune of holding a female body' (1988, 303). Nor, finally, does Spivak fail to point out that the alleged purity of spiritual intentions might well be compromised by far more mundane and mercurial motives. Quoting Kane, Spivak points out:

In Bengal [the fact that] the widow of a sonless member even in a joint Hindu family is entitled to practically the same rights over joint family property which her deceased husband would have had . . . must have frequently induced the surviving members to get rid of the widow by appealing at a most distressing hour to her devotion to and love for her husband. (1988, 300)

Spivak draws on the two steps of deconstruction, reversal and displacement (see Derrida, 1981b), in order to describe the sense in which Bhubaneswari Bhaduri 'perhaps rewrote the social text of *sati* suicide in an interventionist way' (1999, 307). In the first instance, she reverses 'the interdict against a menstruating widow's right to immolate herself' by waiting 'for the onset of menstruation' (307). In the second place, this reversal is also a displacement of sati as 'the sanctioned motive for female suicide' (307). Spivak reads this overturning of a taboo (the interdiction of sati for the ostensibly 'unclean,' menstruating woman) as a subaltern displacement of sati. If the suicide of one who would protest British rule in India is in some sense a mute protest, a silenced rebellion, in another sense it is a graphic re-inscription of a traditional Hindu practice, one that stages the body as the scene of writing, inscribing on the corpse of a woman the aberrant excesses of imperial, colonial history. Spivak claims that even the example she chooses is one that refrains from constructing the subaltern with any purity.

'Bhubaneswari Bhaduri was not a "true" subaltern. She was a woman of the middle class, with access, however clandestine, to the bourgeois movement for Independence' (1999, 308). Spivak comments, 'I was not, in fact, choosing a distinctly subaltern person. This woman was middle class. Thus I implied that, in the case of the woman, the idea of subalternity, because of woman's limited permission to narrate, becomes contaminated' (Landry and Maclean 1996, 289).

In an interview, attempting to explain what she meant when she wrote 'the subaltern cannot speak' (1998, 20), following a number of critical responses, Spivak observes that

> By 'speaking' I was obviously talking about a transaction between the speaker and the listener. That is what did not happen in the case of a woman who took her own body at the moment of death to inscribe a certain kind of undermining – too weak a word – a certain kind of annulment of all the propositions that underlie the regulative psychobiography that underwrites *sati* . . . And even that incredible effort to speak did not fulfill itself in a

speech act. And therefore, in a certain kind of rhetorical anguish after the accounting of this, I said, 'the subaltern cannot speak!' (1996, 289)

Revisiting this 'passionate lament' in her *Critique of Postcolonial Reason*, Spivak concedes it was 'inadvisable' (1999, 308), and goes on to acknowledge that Abena Busia, one of her critics, was 'right, of course' (309) in pointing out that Spivak herself is 'able to read Bhubaneswari's case, and therefore she *has* spoken in some way . . . All speaking, even seemingly the most immediate, entails a distanced decipherment by another, which is, at best, an interception. That is what speaking is' (309). Following this concession, Spivak does not exactly take it back, but proceeds to caution that 'the moot decipherment by another in an academic institution (willy-nilly a knowledge-production factory) many years later must not be too quickly identified with the "speaking" of the subaltern' (309).

Spivak's emphasis is thus to resist two equally ideologically mistaken assumptions. First, she distances herself from the idea that the subaltern or oppressed subject is 'naturally articulate' (1988, 289), with the consequence that all the intellectual has to do is to channel the inherent truth represented by the subaltern, who thereby becomes an unproblematized, anthropological, native informant, with direct access to some unmediated truth. In this scenario, the intellectual falls into the trap of representing themselves as a 'transparent' (1988, 275) vessel able to transmit some transcendent and inconstestable (perhaps spiritual) truth. This is the position she attributes to Foucault and Deleuze, whose transparency is 'produced' (1988, 279), a production that passes itself off as transparent, in a gesture that is in fact far from disinterested, a production that masks their implication in all the exploitative processes by which the first world maintains its supremacy over the third world. The more the intellectual refuses such an implication, the more Spivak points out the incoherence of any claim to be disinterested. Second, Spivak distances herself from the idea that, out of fear of misrepresentation, the only viable solution for the intellectual is to avoid the problem entirely – which would entail, in this context, neglecting or dismissing *en masse* the entire problem of the subaltern – by abstaining from any attempt to represent others, or to say anything at all meaningful about oppression (see 1988, 286). It is inadequate to set up the subaltern as somehow containing all the answers to a revolutionary consciousness, as if all the intellectual had to do were passively receive and interpret, without transforming, a pure, authentic experience. This both completely avoids the problem of what used to be called good old-fashioned false consciousness, which now, filtered through the work of Althusser, gets dubbed ideology – isn't the genius of capitalism that it reproduces itself not merely at the level of materiality, but also at the level of ideology? – while also sidestepping the question of what useful role the intellectual plays. If we presume that the subaltern speaks the truth, isn't the need for intellectuals obviated, or at least reduced to the role of indifferent communicator of a previously completed truth?

It is, then, inadequate for the intellectual to wash her hands entirely of the question of acute ideological repression with all its messy difficulties, by refusing to engage it as an issue at all. Such a stance ignores the problem altogether, implicitly deeming it as unimportant, attempting to save face or to absolve oneself from the possibility of misrepresentation, or complicity. Equally, it is inadequate to merely appeal directly to naïve experience in order to construct it as the 'truth.' Striving to chart a path between these two extremes, Spivak refuses to romanticize or idealize the subaltern. 'I think people . . . go wrong, and this is very much a United States' phenomenon, in thinking that we have any interest in preserving subalternity' (Landry and Maclean 1996, 289). Beyond the problematic of the subaltern as such, Spivak is concerned to etch out the double effacement suffered by the subaltern woman. 'If, in the context of colonial production, the subaltern has no history and cannot speak, the subaltern as female is even more deeply in shadow' (1988, 287). Doubly eclipsed, first by colonialism, and then by a reactive Indian nationalism, the motif of the subaltern woman serves to remind us not only of the complicity between two great political systems of oppression, but, just as urgently, of the persistent vigilance required by well-meaning postcolonialists and feminists alike in order not to unthinkingly reinscribe in new guises precisely the kind of marginalization under protest. This does not mean that we can retain a position of innocence or purity, even with our best intentions. It means we must be willing, before all else, to admit to, and submit to examination, our own complicity in systematic oppressions, which cannot be wished away, but which must be thought through – again and again, since cycles of oppression have an uncanny way of reproducing themselves.

CHAPTER 6

PSYCHOANALYTIC AND POSTSTRUCTURALIST FEMINIST THEORY, AND DELEUZIAN RESPONSES

In this chapter, I begin by considering psychoanalytic feminist theory, and then go on to look at the importance of Derrida's formulation of binary oppositions for feminism. I then turn briefly to a Deleuzian feminist critique of both psychoanalytically inspired feminist theory and poststructuralist theory. Finally, using Moira Gatens as my principal reference point, I shall show how the inspirational role that Benedict de Spinoza has provided for Deleuze and Guattari has helped to move feminist theory beyond a Cartesian reference point that has become somewhat sterile.

Abigail Bray and Clare Colebrook take up the practice of anorexia in order to illustrate the limitations of what they call corporeal feminism, and the advantages of a Deleuzian framework (1998). I shall draw on their analysis, which serves a useful purpose, even while it might overlook some of the differences between the various theorists they label corporeal feminists. Bray and Colebrook highlight a general problem with critiques of 'phallocentrism,' that is, with feminist theories that tend to construct an overarching narrative of masculine biased accounts of subjectivity and experience, posited as negatively determining and limiting any expression of female authenticity. In so far as such accounts generalize patriarchal thought as if it formed a monolithic bloc, and continue to see all meaning as emanating from a hegemonic 'symbolic,' they fail to eschew what Nietzsche regarded as reactive thinking. By blaming the enemy – men in general, or the patriarchal way of thinking, or the phallocentric system of meaning – feminism is in danger of merely occupying a negative position, one that mimics the resentful, bitter recrimination of the Judeo-Christian mindset, denigrating this worldly life as one of suffering, producing guilt, and occupying a position of bad conscience. In this case, the accusation goes: men are at fault for making our lives miserable; they are to blame for the fact that we have internalized negative body images; the patriarchal–capitalist media system is at fault for bombarding our consciousness with idealized images of femininity that are impossible to realize, and in relation to which real women will inevitably fall short. It is therefore not women's fault that we are subject to eating disorders such as anorexia or bulimia, but the fault of the media which makes us feel inadequate. To occupy such a stance is to agree to cast oneself as victim, as overdetermined by an all powerful oppressor, or, in Nietzsche's terms, to adopt a slave morality. Instead of aligning itself with reactive or oppositional thinking, feminism should commit itself to creating new sites of meaning, inventing new ways of thinking, and producing innovative concepts. It should be life-affirming, rather than reactionary (see Deleuze 1983). It is not that I think Bray and Colebrook's sometimes sweeping critique of corporeal feminism is entirely fair (indeed I align myself with some aspects of so-called corporeal feminism), but I do think it highlights a tendency of which feminism needs to be aware, and I find compelling the optimism and creativity of Deleuzian-inspired feminist theory. Bray and Colebrook effectively articulate the need for feminist theory to be wary of recreating precisely the kind of grand narratives to which such theories object (although they themselves might be said to fall prey to such a critique in their over-general characterization of corporeal feminism). It might be worth recalling in this context Butler's observation about Luce Irigaray. If Irigaray tends to 'mime the grandiosity of the philosophical errors that she underscores' perhaps 'a hyperbolic rejoinder is necessary when a given injury has remained unspoken for too long' (Butler 1993, 36–7). If patriarchy's denigration of women, which philosophy has been quick to condone, calls for Irigaray's tactical mimesis, the question is how effectively such a hyperbolic response has played itself out in those influenced by Irigaray, and how far it continues to create new blindspots – covering over the salience of racial difference, for example.

Irigaray and Kristeva are two of the most interesting theorists to have worked through the interconnections of feminist theory to psychoanalysis on the one hand and post-Hegelian European philosophy on the other. Since I have laid out in some detail my understanding of Irigaray's contribution to feminist theory elsewhere

(Chanter 1995), I will focus here on Kristeva's contribution. (Other important feminist theorists include Jessica Benjamin [1990], whose work I shall not be able to address here.) Kristeva effects a kind of *rapprochement* between psychoanalytic and linguistic categories. She refers to a body of psychoanalytic work in a way that assumes knowledge of it, not always unpacking the Freudian and Lacanian assumptions that inform the positions she is briefly outlining, while at the same time revising in her own way. It might be helpful then, initially, to lay out a number of distinctions at work: Saussure's signifier/signified distinction, or the symbol and that which is symbolized; Lacan's symbolic/imaginary/real; and Kristeva's own semiotic/symbolic distinction. The latter distinction does not map neatly onto Lacan's tripartite scheme, but is roughly equivalent to Freud's pre-Oedipal/Oedipal distinction, with the proviso that at stake in Kristeva's distinction between the semiotic and the symbolic is the signifying process. For Freud, on the other hand, the transition from the pre-Oedipal to the Oedipal is developmental, but not particularly tied to linguistic competence, except for the brief interlude of the *fort-da* game (see Freud 1953), and even here Freud's emphasis is on repetition and mastery rather than on language learning.

In developing the distinction between the semiotic and the symbolic, Kristeva is responding to, yet also taking further, Lacan's inscription (via Lévi-Strauss) of Freud's two topographies with reference to Saussurean linguistics and Hegelian dialectics, by interrogating in greater detail than did Lacan the pre-Oedipal realm. (There are many good sources on Saussure's influence on Lacan, so I will not repeat that work here; the reader would do well to consult the first chapter of Beardsworth [2004], for example.) The 'first' Freudian topography is organized around the distinctions between unconscious, preconscious, and consciousness, and the second is that of the id, ego, and superego. If Lacan's return to Freud is informed by his taking up of Saussurean linguistics and selective application of Hegelian categories (see Hegel, 1977), Kristeva's emphasis of the pre-Oedipal phase is undertaken in the light of Melanie Klein's development of Freud. In this sense, Kristeva executes another return to Freud, one mediated by Lacan's application of Saussurean and Hegelian concepts and terminology to the Freudian corpus, but one that also elaborates the pre-Oedipal more finely than Lacan. For us, the significance of this renewed attention to the pre-Oedipal is its potential for reassessing the relative importance of the role of the maternal, vis-à-vis the paternal function, and the consequent implications such a rethinking has for what Kristeva will refer to as the totalizing effects of Lacanian discourse. How might Kristeva's redrawing of the psychoanalytic map play out in terms of the authority of the phallus, the sanctity of the castration complex, and the centrality of the Oedipus complex? How, in turn, might these developments impact and inform the possibilities of revolutionary thinking, and what might such possibilities amount to in an era of globalized capitalism and digitalized information systems, an era in which the mass movements of Marxist vanguards no longer serve as a viable model for political agitation and transformation?

The watershed dividing both the semiotic from the symbolic (or in Freudian terms the pre-Oedipal from the Oedipal) is the Lacanian mirror stage, which is read in tandem with the Freudian discovery of castration. The Freudian distinction between the pre-Oedipal and Oedipal could be said to correspond in some sense to the divide between Lacan's differentiation between the imaginary and the symbolic, but with the following important qualification: it leaves aside the question of the Real, which might be understood as functioning in a way that is akin to that part of Kristeva's semiotic, the 'residues' (Kristeva 1984, 49), that are not taken up, or raised up by the symbolic, remaining resistant to signification, even while facilitating (as part of the semiotic) the signifying process. The real might be thought of as the unrepresentable, as that which cannot be thought or incorporated by the symbolic, that which resists signification, exceeds representation, refuses sublation, and which therefore remains in excess of the master signifier (the phallus), the meaning around which language comes to organize itself. In this sense, the real is outside representation, impervious to the signs that circulate in the system of exchange that constitutes the symbolic world. It is the unthinkable, that which cannot be assimilated or integrated into a meaningful system of discourse – hence its association with trauma. For Lacan, trauma is typically associated with the castration complex – for the boy castration anxiety plays out as the fear of losing the penis, and for the girl it plays out as penis-envy – and is read in terms of the prohibitions and cultural prescriptions associated with the Oedipus complex. Castration anxiety comes to stand retrospectively for all other potentially traumatic instances, for any other threatened loss, including that of the fragmented body. By developing the discourse of abjection, the principal resonance of which concerns the infant's need to separate itself from the maternal function, on which its initial prematurity makes it dependent, Kristeva focuses on the threat of total annihilation as an instance of loss that occurs prior to castration anxiety, and that cannot be entirely recuperated within its register. The infant's very existence is at stake in abjection (and not just the potential loss of a phallic sign).

In the background of Kristeva's appropriation, and re-signification of Lacan's return to Freud, is the way that Lacan takes up not only Saussure's distinction between the signifier/signified, but also Hegel's understanding of desire, as distinct from demand and need. There is a progression from need, through demand, to desire, a progression that reflects Lacan's taking up of these Hegelian terms. Desire, for Lacan, as is well known, is always desire for the desire of the other, the desire for recognition. As is also well known, Lacan took up Kojève's reading of Hegel's master-slave relationship, as a lens through which he refracted and truncated the Hegelian path of the dialectic. Demand then, is that which is addressed to the mother by the child, whereas desire is that which appears after the discovery of castration, at which point the child recognizes that it cannot satisfy the mother's desire. In Lacanian terms, the mother's desire lies elsewhere, or in Freudian terms, the Oedipal father is that towards which the mother's desire is directed. As Kristeva will put it in *Tales of Love* (in terms that are less insistent on the heterosexist resonance that infuse the texts of Freud and Lacan) whatever the desire of the mother turns out to be, it is in any case not me (1987).

The Hegelian transition from consciousness to self-consciousness provides the context for understanding how Lacan takes up desire in relation to the other. Just as, for Hegel, what is at stake in the master/ slave dialectic is the recognition of the other, so for Lacan, desire is always the desire of the other. Similarly, just as for Hegel the master/ slave dialectic is a matter of life and death, since the struggle for freedom can turn into a struggle to the death, so the death drive (as well as eros, the life drive, or the drive for self-preservation) is implicated in the psychic struggle that each of us undergoes in our effort to assert our independence (separate from the mother). Each of us is destined to overcome our dependent, infantile state, in which we are little more than a bundle of needs and demands, and to attain subjectivity, a transition which is accomplished in large part through our acquiescence to the law, our subjection to the taboos and prohibitions of the social/symbolic realm. The first such taboo is the incest taboo, played out around the body of the mother. The 'Other' in Lacanian terms is the paternal function or metaphor, which represents the paternal, prohibiting law, the law that governs the symbolic – the law that enjoins the child to observe the mother's desire for the father. This Other takes the place of the mother, or 'is no longer the mother (from whom the child ultimately separates through the mirror stage and castration)' (Kristeva 1984, 48). In other words, the child's entry into the symbolic, and all the social constraints it entails, is structured according to a prohibition regarding the mother. The boy must substitute for his attachment to the mother a future attachment to another woman, who will become his wife. He must confine his libido (previously polymorphous, that is, not yet distinguishing between the progressive stages that Freud identifies as characteristic of maturing sexuality – anal, oral, or phallic pleasure) to the genital, and reserve his sexual attentions to women who are not his mother. The girl must both (on Freud's heterosexually normative, misguided, and outdated account) exchange one erotogenic zone for another, the clitoris for the vagina, and exchange her attachment to the mother for an attachment not with another woman, but with a man, her future husband. The phallus, as symbolic of power, comes to be emblematic of the signifying system, as its master signifier. It represents the paternal order, in that the father is the one whose authority informs the law prohibiting access to the mother.

For Hegel there is a difference in the point of view of how consciousness comes to understand itself (the naïve standpoint) and the point of view of the 'we,' the reader who, having traced the development of consciousness throughout *The Phenomenology of Spirit*, has passed through all the stages of determinate negation, and can look back on these stages, as so many historical shapes of consciousness, from the standpoint of completion. In the same way, there is a difference between the subject considered from two different points of view in psychoanalytic parlance. In fact, even to refer to a 'subject' in the pre-Oedipal or semiotic phase is to borrow the language of the post-Oedipal or symbolic phase. The subject comes to be structured by desire, rather than needs or demands, only after having passed through, or undergone the trauma of, castration (castration anxiety, or penis-envy). That is, the child's realization that the mother's desire lies elsewhere, or that her desire is for the phallus. On the one hand, there is the developmental point of view of the child, who, prior to the mirror stage and discovery of castration (or, in Kristeva's terms, prior to the thetic phase), is prelinguistic, has not yet attained a mastery over language, or has not yet entered into the symbolic – and yet who is immersed in a world that is always already linguistic. On the other hand, there is the point of view of the linguistic subject, who is always already immersed in the symbolic, who, as an acculturated subject, has taken on the social constraints and the normative values embedded in language as a system of signs.

As members of the community of language-users, the task of theorists – including theorists of the semiotic – is inevitably to broach an analysis from the point of view of the symbolic. The task of analyzing the semiotic will therefore necessarily be a reconstructive, retroactive task, one that presupposes the fixity of terms, the stability conferred by the permanence that language confers on ideas. To put this another way is to acknowledge the 'liminary' (Kristeva 1984, 30) or 'boundary' (48) character of language considered from the point of view of syntactical, linguistic signs, where according to the conventions of language usage, certain representations have acquired a permanence, certain values have stabilized and become fixed; yet beneath the fixity of language, a dynamic, unstable domain the topology of which is defined according to drives, primary processes (condensation and displacement, metaphor and metonymy, needs and demands) is in process. This is the significance of Kristeva's critique of formal linguistics as preoccupied with surface phenomena, and neglectful of the deep, diachronic structures that prepare the subject for language. The object of formal linguistics, according to this point of view, is sclerotic, fetishized; its procedures are necrophilic, treating language as a system of signs already set in place, as if meanings were fixed or unassailable, as if thoughts were static, as if the study of signs were an archival or archaeological affair (see Kristeva 1984, 13) – in short, as if language were dead, instead of living and capable of transgression. Putting into question the language of totalization, the transcendental, the absolute, or the theological, Kristeva conceives of the thetic as 'permeable' (63) or pervious – as that which can be transgressed. Hence, Kristeva suggests that the Lacanian 'phallus totalizes the effects of signifieds as having been produced by the signifier' (47), asking whether Lacan 'transcendentalizes semiotic motility, setting it up as a transcendental Signifier?' (48). At the same time as putting into question the totalizing effects of the phallus, Kristeva also recognizes the necessity of 'a completion [finition], a structuration, a kind of totalization of semiotic motility' (51). Without 'verbal expression,' experience would be 'chaotic and inexpressible' (Lévi-Strauss quoted by Kristeva 1984, 244 n.56). For Kristeva, however, rather than the repression of the semiotic in the setting up of a pure signifier, the thetic must be 'taken on or undergone' as a 'position' (51). For Kristeva then, it is not a matter of a refusal, evasion, or repression of 'imaginary castration,' but of construing the thetic (the inception of signification, understood in terms of the mirror stage and castration) as a 'traversable boundary' (51). If castration cannot be evaded, neither is it a matter of 'a castration imposed once and for all, perpetuating the well-ordered signifier and positing it as sacred and unalterable within the enclosure of the Other' (51). In fact, for Kristeva, it is precisely the mobility of the process of signification that should capture our attention, a process that only comes to be stabilized in a final stage, which is preceded by a period of language acquisition taken by Kristeva to be of paramount importance. The instability of the process of language acquisition can never entirely be put to rest, and returns as a 'disturbance of language and/or of the order of the signifier' and even 'destroys the symbolic' (50). That is, the irruption of the semiotic is capable of effecting a revolution, renewal, or rejuvenation of the symbolic order, which is itself only possible on the basis of the semiotic.

Presided over by maternal regulation, the semiotic or pre-Oedipal is characterized by stases and discontinuities, waves of activity and passivity, charges of energy, absences and presences, but there are as yet no firm distinctions between subject and object (or world), me and you, inner and outer. Thus, even though we designate the function to which needs and wants are harnessed 'maternal,' it is crucial to remember that such designations proceed according to the symbolic realm, or the paternal law, which has already decided in favor of certain privileges, not the least of which is the importance of symbolic castration, as marking the entry into language. That is, even though the pre-Oedipal or semiotic is specified with regard to the maternal function, such a function is operational *for the child* in a way that precedes the discovery of castration, and as such precedes the discovery of sexual difference. Sexual difference, that is to say, is assigned retroactively. The specification of the semiotic as regulated by the maternal body is a specification that proceeds from the symbolic, from the point of view of the subject who has passed through the thetic phase, or who has entered into the symbolic, a subject who has taken on the discovery of castration, who has submitted to the law of sexual difference. For the child, however (just as for the naïve consciousness in Hegel), no such distinction is possible, prior to the entry into the symbolic. The mother can be differentiated from the father only from the point of view of the symbolic order, only from the point of view of a subject who has taken on the ordeal of castration anxiety.

The mirror stage, Kristeva emphasizes, produces the 'spatial intuition' that consists of the separation of the child from its image, and is 'at the heart of signification – in signs and in sentences' (46). In this regard it is worth noting that Lacan tends to emphasize the temporal aspect – the salutary affect that the mirror image has on the child from the point of view of anticipating a future autonomy, not yet granted by the fragmentation of the body due to its prematurity, and consequent lack of motor-coordination (see Beardsworth 2004). The discovery of castration completes the process of separation that posits a subject as signifiable, that is, as separate, as confronted by another. 'Castration puts the finishing touches on the process of separation that posits the subject as signifiable, which is to say, separate, always confronted by an other: *imago* in the mirror (signified) and semiotic process (signifier)' (Kristeva 1984, 47). Lacan designates this moment the 'aha' moment in the 'The Mirror Stage,' a moment of recognition when the child finds itself as other, in the mirror. It both is and is not the image in the mirror (see Lacan 1977). At an age between six and eighteen months, the child is not yet able to stand on its own, without support, or to control its movement very well. In this sense, the child is fragmented at the corporeal level, and yet the image it seizes in the mirror is stable, perfected, complete. For this reason, Lacan sees it as heralding a future autonomy, holding out the promise of an independence that has not yet arrived, but which the child anticipates by way of a mirage. The mirror image is both facilitating and alienating, both salutary and inhibiting. On the one hand it presents the child with an image to which its fragmented, dependent state does not yet conform, while on the other, it holds out the fate of what is still to come.

The question for feminists is, if the socio-symbolic order is governed by a patriarchally conceived father, how is it possible to transgress this order? Artistic practice, or more specifically, poetic language, plays an important role in Kristeva's answer. Art, for

Kristeva, is a confrontation with the boundary separating nature or animality from culture or humanity. Thus, the artistic practices that are played out around the sacrifice of the father by the primal horde, a sacrifice that, according to Freud, founds culture, are capable of miming, or re-enacting the shift from pre-history to society. In this sense, as a confrontation with the transition from nature to culture, and at the same time as a confrontation with the materiality of the body (sacrificed animal or human), art facilitates a rethinking of that boundary. That is, it both allows access to the drives that are repressed by the inauguration of the incest taboo, which puts off-limits the availability of certain women, and it mimics the institution of this taboo. As such, art can provide a locale in which the founding taboos of culture can be confronted, and perhaps transformed, reworked, revolutionized. This is not to say that all art is politically radical in its effect, only that it can be transformative, precisely insofar as it re-visits the founding moment of culture. Art can equally well be a site of complicity with the cultural codes in operation, a means of supporting hegemonic codes. When art aligns itself with the prevailing modes of authority in a given culture, far from demonstrating that these particular symbolic codes (patriarchal, sexist, heterosexist) are not the only codes available, it puts its weight behind them, and conceals the revolutionary potential that the artist's confrontation with the founding moment of culture harbors within it. When art opens up culture to the energies that are typically closed off or repressed when we unquestioningly follow the taboos that society sanctions – such as the taboo on homosexuality – its revolutionary force is unleashed.

The significance Kristeva attributes to art is attached to the significance of artistic practices (ritual, dance, etc.) that accompany sacrifice, which (following Freud) she takes to be the foundational moment of any society. Art confronts the border between animality and humanity, by revisiting that founding moment in which humans separate from nature. It thereby embraces the specificity of their humanity, the capacity to abide by law, the setting up of a social order in which to be human is not to blindly submit to drives, to be guided solely by the pleasure principle, but to defer pleasure, to acquiesce to the reality principle, to follow the law. Art mimes the movement of the inception of symbolic economy, so that the transition from animality to humanity is re-enacted. It is worth noting, then, that Kristeva's view of art does not equate it with ritual as such; the function of art is to renegotiate the way in which the boundary between nature and culture is drawn. As such, art participates in the political in a way that could be thought in tandem with the transition that Walter Benjamin outlines from art as ritual to art as political (see Benjamin 1968). The age of mechanical reproduction transforms art, so that it is no longer defined by its aura, in which the uniqueness of the work of art is at stake, and in which the public has to rely on experts to explain to them the significance of the work. With the emergence of photography, and especially with film, not only does art become reproducible, so that images are instantaneously beamed into the cinema, but the viewing public takes on the role of critic. In fact, the mass consumption of film both appeals to the status quo, and makes possible its subversion: we can all become armchair critics.

For Kristeva, the re-enacting of the movement from a state of nature to the symbolic exchange that takes place under some kind of social contract – some agreed upon values around which a community coheres – provides access to a realm that is cut off from the symbolic when that realm is treated as if its inception were theological, as if the social order appeared *ex nihilo*, as if the thetic break wherein symbolic relations are formed were transcendental, as if there were not a deep structure, a generative process. The domain of the semiotic first sets in motion what later becomes susceptible to the law of exchange, a system of symbolic equivalences that constitutes the meaningfulness of signs, or the setting up of language. Such a miming – not of objects whose meaning is already settled but of the process by which any meaning becomes possible, a foundational process that involves setting ourselves off from the chaos of nonsense, demarcating ourselves from nature, animality, and mere obedience to drives – harbors within it a disruptive potential. Precisely insofar as it acknowledges that which society casts aside, poetic language, as a miming of the inauguration of the symbolic order, putting us in touch with elements whose destructive potential has been tamed and ordered according to the symbolic law.

The heterogeneity of the flow of language is only accessible from the point of view of a subject who has taken on the trauma of castration, who has submitted to the law of sexual difference, and positioned herself or himself in relation to that law – in other words, a subject who has entered into language, who has been situated in relationship to the rules and regulations of society. Heterogeneity can only be posited from within the symbolic, from the symbolic side of the semiotic/symbolic divide. To speak of the semiotic is always necessarily to do so from the position of the symbolic, and yet Kristeva is at pains to emphasize that the semiotic is not entirely subject to the laws of sublation: there is a remainder, a semiotic residue that remains resistant to language, and cannot be taken up adequately within symbolic terms, cannot be made homologous with meaning. There is a paradoxical quality to the semiotic/symbolic distinction. On the one hand, the semiotic aims at meaning, indeed it must be translated into meaningful signs in order to exist, yet on the other hand, once this translation is effected, its limitations become evident. While the permanence of language is what provides access to the semiotic, the instability of the semiotic eludes that permanence, and is capable of issuing challenges to its authority, challenges that can transform and even destroy meaning. This is the revolutionary charge of poetic language.

Kristeva notes the slippage in Lévi-Strauss and Lacan, such that there is no room for a proper differentiation between the idea that we must all enter a symbolic system, become speaking beings, capable of making ourselves understood within a given system of language, and the idea that we must all enter the particular symbolic system associated with the Oedipus and castration complexes. As Kristeva puts it, the discovery of castration 'makes the phallic function a symbolic function – *the* symbolic function' (1984, 47). Differentiating herself from this position, Kristeva reads the thetic break, which she parses out in terms of the mirror stage and the discovery of castration, not as if its status were theological: the thetic break does not come out of nowhere; it is a boundary that is permeable, and we are capable of traversing it, not in order merely to recuperate the semiotic from which it separates us, but also to return to the semiotic in order to take it up in a new way. One form that the theologization of the thetic takes is the 'subordination' of the signifying process 'to the social relations between subjects caught in kinship relations' (1984, 78). An example of such subordination – and its exemplary status is crucial for us, both because it specifies the order of problems that the Lacanian notion of the symbolic and its celebration of meaning as phallic has posed for feminist theorists, and because it is the locale of the privileging of sexual difference – is the 'exchange of women,' as a means of society's 'self-regulation' (1984, 72). By refusing to accept the theological status of the thetic break, Kristeva opens up a space in which to interrogate the sleight of hand by which, for Lévi-Strauss and Lacan, *a* symbolic economy becomes *the* symbolic economy, an economy, then, which rests upon the circulation of women as gifts, the subordination of women to a kinship system that is not merely sexist, but also heterosexist. The kinship laws that are set in place in acknowledgment of a taboo on the maternal body, an incest taboo, are thereby capable of transgression. Paternal authority is not absolute; the father, who enshrines the law, the prohibition against incest, which puts the mother's body off limits, marks the place of the mother's desire, and in doing so, construes the mother's desire according to normative constraints. This construction of the symbolic construes subjectivity in reference to a universalized masculine ideal, and desire as heterosexual.

Just as Kristeva contests the significance of the Lacanian symbolic, so she shifts the emphasis away from the phallus as transcendental signifier. While some kind of thetic break is necessary, while some kind of totalizing system must have been set in place, Kristeva emphasizes both its necessity – its decisive, vigorous character – and at the same time its lability. Kristeva is not so much interested in confirming the centrality of the Saussurean distinction between the signifier/signified as she is in displacing it, or rather showing how that distinction comes to usurp an operation that in fact facilitates it, namely the distinction of the semiotic from the symbolic. Internal to, and constitutive of the symbolic system, the signifier/signified distinction can only be put in place on the basis of another, prior, operation, one that the theological stance toward the thetic break covers over. The semiotic (rhythmic, musical, tonal) dimension of language is transformed into a signifier, raised up to the symbolic, where it takes on the representative function of designating, symbolizing, signifying. Theories of language which take this function of designation or naming to cover the entire domain of the signifying process fall into the trap of treating language as if it were a reified, fetishized system, in which meanings are given, stable and self-evident, whereas for Kristeva, to treat language as a system of signs is merely to take account of a liminal, or boundary moment of its production, while neglecting the process that gives rise to signification, and which returns to disturb its order.

While the work of Luce Irigaray (1985) is certainly very different from that of Kristeva's in many respects, the two share at least two important aspects in common. Both of them are strongly influenced by (yet also critical of) Freudo-Lacanian psychoanalytic theory, and both of them posit the feminine as a privileged other that nourishes and yet is excluded from the order of representation. Influenced by Derrida in this respect, Irigaray is critical of the 'phallogocentric' economy of western metaphysics – that is, critical of the way in which the phallus functions as a token of male privilege, and critical of the way it functions in tandem with a 'logos' that makes that privilege central to the ways we understand and conceive of ourselves and the world. The Greek word 'logos' can be translated in many ways (including law, word, reason, and logic). We are familiar with how it is taken up in the words 'psychology' or 'sociology' to mean study of the psyche or study of society. To say that western thinking is phallogocentric, then, is to say that it takes as its standard, as if it were the law, the regulation of the phallus, making it central to the interpretation of all meaning. To quote Ellen K. Feder and Emily Zakin:

> The concept of phallogocentrism makes clear the connection between the valuation of presence and the phallicized Symbolic Order. It thus designates that operation by which logocentrism constructs binary, hierarchical categories whose dominant terms are marked as masculine and whose masculine terms are marked as dominant. From a feminist perspective, phallogocentrism can be read as the production of intelligible experience through exclusive categories which privilege the siting of a masculinized perspective. Phallogocentrism makes clear the contrast between the idea of a full, present, apparent phallus and that of the castrated woman, who lacks a phallus, has nothing to be seen, and who therefore represents absence needing to be recuperated. (1997, 47)

If western metaphysics has operated by establishing a series of dualisms (mind/body, reason/passions, intellect/matter, transcendent/immanent), it comes as no surprise that these binary ways of thinking have also been gendered: mind, reason, intellect, and transcendence are figured as masculine, while their opposites are figured as feminine. The fact that in order for reason or intellect to maintain their transcendent status, the necessary tasks that are entrusted to women as their 'natural' jobs – caring for affects and emotions, looking after bodily needs – turn out to be essential not only for the maintenance of these oppositions, but for the nourishing and stabilizing of the hierarchy, is often neglected.

Beyond its reference to fundamental, western metaphysical distinctions, Derrida's understanding of how 'binary oppositions' function can also be applied to the way in which, in Joan Scott's words, 'biological theories about sexual difference' function as 'legitimating truths' (1988, 36). Sex operates as the hierarchical term of a 'binary opposition' that affirms the power relationship between sex and gender, rather than displacing it. As Scott says, deconstruction 'shows [dichotomous terms] to be not natural but constructed oppositions, constructed for particular purposes in particular contexts' (1988, 37–8). Or, in the words of Feder and Zakin, 'The appearance of an opposition between man and woman is an effect of ontological categories which, despite their inadequacy in containing identity within their borders, nonetheless succeed in characterizing sexual difference as a binary relation' (1997, 24). The binary oppositions of man/woman or sex/gender are not eternal verities, but rather cultural constructions which derive their normative force from those invested in maintaining a hierarchical order defined by patriarchal, heteronormative power, harnessed for reproductive ends. When feminists confine themselves to railing against such power, they confirm and perpetuate the authority of that hierarchy, rather than disrupting it in a way that leads to new relationships that can create a new order.

There are two steps to a deconstructive strategy: 'the reversal and displacement of binary oppositions,' as Scott puts it (1988, 37). Referring to a series of interviews Derrida gave in *Positions* (1981b) Christie McDonald expands:

In the first phase a reversal was to take place in which the opposed terms would be inverted. Thus woman, as a previously subordinate term, might become the dominant one in relation to man. Yet because such a scheme of reversal could only repeat the traditional scheme (in which the hierarchy of duality is always reconstituted), it alone could not effect any significant change. Change would only occur through the 'second' a more radical phase of deconstruction in which a 'new' concept would be forged simultaneously. (Derrida, 1997, 31–2)

In accordance with his claim in 'Signature, Even, Context,' that 'Deconstruction does not consist in passing from one concept to another, but in overturning and displacing a conceptual order, as well as the nonconceptual order with which the conceptual order is articulated' (Derrida 1982, 329), Derrida goes on to clarify that he does not believe we have a new concept of woman, and that he is 'not sure that [he feels] the lack of it' (1997, 33). Referring to the two steps of deconstruction he had outlined in *Positions*, he adds:

> I am not sure that 'phase two' marks a split with 'phase one,' a split whose form would be a cut along an indivisible line. The relationship between these two phases doubtless has another structure. I spoke of two distinct phases for the sake of clarity, but the relationship of one phase to another is marked less by conceptual determinations . . . than by a transformation or general deformation of logic. (1997, 33)

Derrida explains that so long as sexual difference is understood dialectically, sexual difference is erased, since Hegel's dialectic has always already decided in favor of the 'truth,' which presents itself as universal, while hiding its masculine bias. The feminine remains the secondary term, defined in opposition to the masculine, as not-the-truth, as other. 'One insures phallocentric mastery under the cover of neutralization every time . . . And phallocentrism adorns itself now and then, here and there, with an appendix: a certain kind of feminism' (1997, 34). The kind of feminism that appends itself to phallocentrism is, to use Nietzsche's terms, a ' "reactive" feminism' (1997, 27), or a feminism that remains complicit with patriarchy. In Elizabeth Grosz's words:

> If feminism does not occupy a space outside of patriarchy and phallocentrism, if it is implicated in the interstices of patriarchal functioning, then the security of its identity, the definitiveness of its borders as other than and outside patriarchy, its very self-representations as a bounded position separable from patriarchy are all problematized. (1997, 77)

In this sense, feminism must remain constantly vigilant so that it does not become another form of dogmatism, does not merely copy the kind of authority it seeks to put into question, does not transform itself into a new kind of straitjacket.

Not only is the interdependence of patriarchy and feminism, men and women, or sex and gender shown, but there is also a call to go beyond merely reversing old hierarchies (see Scott 1988, 33). It is therefore not enough for feminists to become militant and powerful, calling all the shots. Feminists must also take a lead in forging a new politics and ethics, new ways of relating to one another, both among women and between men and women. Rather than continuing to adhere to competitive, adversarial relationships, feminism should be experimenting with producing environments in which mutually supportive relations are fostered, in which diversity is prized, and in which negativity is not allowed to rule to day. Creating relationships based upon nurturing novelty is not a matter of falsely claiming that women are better at mutuality or caring or being other-oriented than men – even if historically such tasks have fallen to women. It is rather a matter finding ways of relating, acting, and being that do not fall back into old patterns of *ressentiment*, domination, and competitiveness. It is a question of not being governed by reactionary forces, or negative sentiments, such as fear, jealousy, or insecurity. It is a question of being able and willing to rise above such affects, rather than letting them spiral out of control. It is a question of being affirmative, and creative, rather than reacting out of being threatened, thereby continuing a cycle of hostility and marginalization, in which men are targeted as oppressors, or racial minorities become the dumping ground for white, feminist frustration.

Feminist critiques of phallogocentrism have been seen as reactive by Deleuzian feminists, who argue against the tendency to produce one more grand narrative, as if one story fits the experience of diverse women, and as if the privilege of sexual difference were built into the very structure of subjectivity, rendering racial or class differences necessarily derivative or secondary to sexual difference. As Colebrook asks, 'can feminism be the affirmation of an event and not one more grounding narrative?' (2000, 13). Taking up Nietzsche's celebration of the affirmative, the positive and the active, rather than reactive, Deleuze emphasizes events, singularities, intensities, and flows in a discourse that is anti-representationalist. For Deleuze and Guattari, the 'only question is how anything works, with its intensities, flows, processes, partial objects . . . What matters is whether it works, and how it works, and who it works for' (Deleuze 1995, 22). In an interesting critique of what they call 'corporeal feminism' – in which they include Butler (1993), Rosi Braidotti (1994),

Teresa Brennan (1993), Rosalyn Diprose (1994), Robyn Ferrell (1991), Elizabeth Grosz (1994), and Moira Gatens (1996) – Bray and Colebrook argue that these theorists have been led astray by an excessive emphasis on representation, a continued adherence (even in resisting it) to an ultimately still Cartesian dichotomy between mind and matter, or representation and materiality, and a reactive attitude towards patriarchy. This version of feminism remains beholden to a Hegelian legacy, even as it tries to overcome it. As a result, it construes the maternal-feminine as the repressed, negated, or excluded other of phallic thought. According to corporeal feminism, patriarchy imposes idealized representations of beauty, equated in this culture with thinness, such representations are internalized, and as a result, eating disorders such as anorexia are read as resulting from pernicious, patriarchal capitalist practices, which control women's body images as much as they control patterns of consumption. What we want – and don't want – derives directly from our being conditioned by unrealizable ideals of femininity that saturate the market in the form of the commodified, airbrushed beauty of supermodels. As Bray and Colebrook point out, such an understanding assumes that consumers of idealized images of femininity are not only passive, but also incapable of creativity. Reading such theorists as influenced by Irigaray, they propose a Deleuzian reading of anorexia that refuses to see the anorexic body as pathological, as opposed to some ostensibly normal body image, which is assumed to be authentic. Taking up Deleuze's insistence that there is no general body, and no single theory, Bray and Colebrook suggest that the anorexic body should not be seen as a pathological response to phallocentric representations of women's bodies, but as a creative event, in a network of other events. They call for a 'specific grammar' of anorexic practices, such as 'calorie counting,' 'weighing and measuring the body,' and 'various dietetic regimens,' claiming that 'there are no anorexics, only activities of dietetics, measuring, regulation, and calculation' (1998, 62). 'The anorexic body could be seen as an intensity occurring within a positive field of production. This field would not be an isolated object for analysis (the anorexic) but an event connected to other events (this practice, with this effect, with this practice, with this connection, with this body, with this sign, etc.)' (63). Showing a concern for singularity, Bray and Colebrook distance themselves both from psychoanalytic theories, which posit the phallus as the principal signifier of the body, and from postructuralist analyses that read the body merely as a sign. While Deleuze and Guattari, like Nietzsche, endorse the idea of the unconscious, they do not restrict its interpretation to the Oedipus complex. To do so is to domesticate the libido (see Deleuze, 1995, 16–17). As Rosi Braidotti says, 'Deleuze defines the unconscious as a productive, forward propelling force of flows or intensities' (2000, 161). For Deleuze, 'The unconscious isn't a theater but a factory, a productive machine, and the unconscious isn't playing around all the time with mummy and daddy but with races, tribes, continents, history and geography, always some social frame' (Deleuze 1995, 144). Deleuze and Guattari see classic psychoanalytic theory as similar to capitalism: both incur infinite debts. In the case of psychoanalysis, it is not credit, but the Oedipus complex that stages an endless debt (see 17 and 181). As Vernena Andermatt Conley puts it, 'Oedipus is a handmaiden to capitalist economy' (2000, 20). For Deleuze and Guattari, psychoanalysis is 'pretty dull and sad as it burbles on about Oedipus, castration, the death instinct and so on' (22). Perhaps the question that remains is how far psychoanalysis is capable of renewing itself, so that it does not continue to perpetrate exclusionary thinking, for it is upon the answer to that question that its continued usefulness depends. Anne McClintock (1995) and Hortense Spillers (1997) are among those whose work addresses this question in productive ways, by opening up psychoanalysis to the discourse of race, in the case of Spillers, and, in the case of McClintock, by pursuing a rigorous analysis of Freud's corpus in the context of race, class, and gender. In particular, McClintock is interested in how colonial discourses constructed desire in hegemonic ways.

Up to this point, although my analysis has been critical of the ways in which a dualistic, Cartesian model has informed some models of the sex/gender distinction, I have not shown how some feminist theorists have been able to move beyond sterile dualisms. In the final part of this chapter, I take my cue from the work of Gatens, and other feminist theorists to have seen the value of Spinoza's critique of Descartes, many of them by utilizing the work of Deleuze and Guattari. Although Gatens is included in the group of feminists that Bray and Colebrook dub 'corporeal feminists,' in fact her engagement of both Spinoza and Deleuze for feminist thinking predates Bray and Colebrook's argument. In addition to moving beyond Cartesian dualism, the track that I plot through Spinoza, Deleuze and Guattari, and feminist theory, emphasizes a new way of thinking the history of philosophy, the need to move beyond models that privilege recognition, and the importance of affirmative, rather than reactive thinking.

At times Deleuze is given to excessive statements, particularly when it comes to describing his relationship to the history of philosophy, as it has been traditionally taught.

'I could not stand Descartes, the dualisms and the Cogito, or Hegel, the triad and the operation of the negation' (Deleuze and Parnet 2002, 14). He belongs, he tells us, to 'one of the last generations' to have been 'more or less bludgeoned to death with the history of philosophy' which 'plays a patently repressive role in philosophy' (Deleuze 1995, 6). Marxism, Freudian psychoanalysis, and Saussurean linguistics are also characterized as repressive: they are the 'new apparatuses of power in thought itself' (Deleuze and Parnet 2002, 14). Deleuze calls the traditional approach to the history of philosophy 'philosophy's own version of the Oedipus complex' (1995, 6). Among other things it is the universalism of systems of thought such as Marxism, which imitates that of its target of critique, capitalism, to which Deleuze and Guattari object (see 1988, 20). This does not mean that he sees his own philosophy as anti-systematic, but rather that he and Guattari see the 'concept of system' itself as having changed (Deleuze and Guattari 1994, 9). Deleuze understands systematicity in an open-ended fashion, or, as Paul Patton says, quoting a remark addressed to Jean-Clet Martin, 'he envisages a "system in perpetual heterogeneity"' (2000, 17). The privileging of heterogeneity or difference over homogeneity and sameness, and the tracing of how concepts come into contact with new problems, giving rise to different configurations, or their iteration in new ways, is treated in one of Deleuze's most important books under the heading *Difference and Repetition*. Concepts 'have their own way of not dying while remaining subject to constraints of renewal, replacement, and mutation that give philosophy a history as well as a turbulent geography' (Deleuze and Guattari 1994, 8). According to Deleuze, philosophy is not contemplation, any more than it is reflection or communication (see 6). Rather, 'the object of philosophy is to create concepts that are always new . . . Concepts are not waiting for us ready-made, like heavenly bodies. There is no heaven for concepts. They must be invented, fabricated, or rather created' (5). There is no Platonic realm of eternal ideas, no truth beyond this world. Philosophy is 'in a perpetual state of digression or digressiveness' (23).

Deleuze's rejection of a certain approach to the history of philosophy should not be taken as an outright condemnation of it. It is a certain, dominant, 'image of thought' (see Patton 2000, ch. 1) to which he objects, according to which the history of philosophy has played the role of 'the agent of power . . . how can you think without having read Plato, Descartes, Kant and Heidegger, and so-and-so's book about them? A formidable school of intimidation which manufactures specialists in thought' (Deleuze and Parnet 2002, 13). His interest lies in those philosophers who provide 'a critique of negativity' and a 'denunciation of power' (Deleuze 1995, 6). The philosophers Deleuze enlists in his alternative anti-representationalist, anti-dualist, anti-moralist, anti-dogmatic view of philosophy have 'escaped' the history of philosophy 'in one respect or altogether: Lucretius, Spinoza, Hume, Nietzsche, Bergson' (Deleuze and Parnet 2002, 14–15). These thinkers are anti-rationalist, affirmative, inventive, creative, productive, and experimental. 'They proceed only through positive, affirmative force' (15). By contrast, the standard history of philosophy:

> stifl[es] all life in seeking an abstract first principle. Whenever one believes in a great first principle, one can no longer produce anything but great, sterile dualisms . . . In fact the first principle is always a mask, a simple image. That does not exist, things do not start to move and come alive until the level of the second, third, fourth principle, and these are no longer even principles. (54–5)

We shall see in a moment that Deleuze interrogates the founding first principle of modern philosophy, namely Descartes' cogito, putting into question whether it does, in fact, constitute the beginning or ground that Descartes constructs it as. Perhaps, suggests Deleuze – who is fond of invoking the 'middle' rather than the first principles of philosophy – it only 'appears to be a beginning' (1994, 129). For now, it should be clear that, as Paul Patton suggests, Deleuze's approach to the history of philosophy is similar to Derrida's in that, far from repudiating it, both of them rewrite it in a sense (see Patton 2000, 15–17). Deleuze even embraces the idea of 'double reading' (1988, 129), a notion that has become a hallmark of Derrida; Deleuze, one might say, does so by writing difference back into the canon.

Deleuze is critical of what he calls the 'model of recognition' characteristic of 'Plato's *Theaetetus*, Descartes' *Meditations*, or Kant's
Critique of Pure Reason' (1994, 134). Since it is his Cartesian
Professor, Alquié – along with the renowned Hegelian scholar
Hyppolite (see Deleuze and Parnet, 2002, 12) – against whom
Deleuze finds it necessary to rebel (we will avoid the claim that he
must kill the father!), let us take Descartes as our example. Our
reasons for doing so are not just biographical; the Cartesian cogito
has found its way into constructions of sex and gender, in addition
to which, as Deleuze and Guattari observe, it is 'one of the best
known signed philosophical concepts' (1994, 24). As such, it can
serve our purposes well. Just as certain philosophical constructions of sex and gender are handed down to us, so we inherit the
following 'signed concepts' which we identify by 'proper names,'
serving as historical markers to designate the 'intrinsic *conceptual
personae*' that 'haunt' concepts (Deleuze and Guattari 1994, 24)
and help to define concepts (see 2): 'Aristotle's substance, Descartes'
cogito, Leibniz's monad, Kant's condition, Schelling's power,
Bergson's duration [*durée*]' (7). Yet these concepts that are signed
by, or created by, certain 'great philosophers' (28) also have a history
(see 18); they do not come out of nowhere. Concepts 'are never
created from nothing' (19). Rather, they emerge out of the becoming-
other of older philosophical concepts, and they are transformed by
having new components introduced to them. Thus whereas in
Descartes, the cogito 'crystallizes' into a concept (26), the Cartesian
cogito is transformed by Kant's version of the cogito through the
explicit introduction of time into the concept of the self as 'I think.'

The Cartesian cogito has, as it were, taken on a life of its own, spaw-
ning all kinds of (perhaps illegitimate, but nonetheless influential)
paradigms for thinking. These include the model for thinking sex and
gender. Sex is taken as a given: male and female bodies are presumed
to exist in and of themselves, with the 'biological' distinction between
male and female serving as a stable ground, onto which can be
mapped, with relative equanimity, the 'social' or behavioural concepts
of masculinity and femininity. As Gatens says: 'The body/mind
dualism associated with Cartesianism, has fed into the sex/gender
dualism where the bodily capacities of each sex are considered to be
relatively fixed (within a given range). Culture, it is allowed, may
influence the final form which gendered subjectivity takes, but only
within the parameters set by nature' (2000, 57; also see Gatens 1996,

1–20). Gatens argues – and this is not so much a response to Bray and Colebrook's critique of corporeal feminism as an anticipation of it – that Deleuze, particularly in taking up Spinoza, provides valuable resources for feminist thought. Dualistic, Cartesian versions of metaphysics on which conceptions of sex and gender are often based – however unselfconsciously or inaccurately – give way to a vision of sexuality that is more open to transgendered identities. The allegedly 'natural' ground of the body becomes a hybrid of the 'artificial' and the 'natural'; bodies are no longer envisaged as a stable, passive ground on which gender is founded. At the same time, in the words of Gatens and Lloyd, Spinoza's 'philosophy allows the modern preoccupation with autonomous individual selfhood to re-connect with Ideals of community, without thereby collapsing hard-won individuality into an all-encompassing, pre-existing collective identity' (1999, 2).

According to Deleuze and Guattari, Spinoza earns the title 'the prince of philosophers' because he is, perhaps (with the exception of Bergson who is 'mature' enough to follow his 'inspiration') the 'only philosopher never to have compromised with transcendence' (1994, 48). It is Spinoza's philosophy of radical immanence, his insistence on an infinitely complex, materialist monism, that has proved so attractive to feminist philosophers such as Gatens and Rosi Braidotti. For Braidotti, 'the notion of radical immanence' provides 'a political edge related to power issues. It also opens critical theory to an ethical and an ecological dimension which embeds the subject in social relations of power. Knowledge claims rest on the immanent structure of subjectivity and must resist the gravitational pull toward abstract transcendentality' (2002, 62). As Gatens says, for Spinoza:

> Rationality is not a transcendent capacity of a disembodied 'mind' but an immanent power of active nature. Neither reason nor law come to us 'from above' but rather develop immanently from our collective situations. Ironically, it is precisely because philosophers often fail to acknowledge the embodiedness of reason and knowledge that their own (embodied) imaginings play such a large part in their 'reasoned' accounts of politics, morality and justice. (1996, 148)

Gatens goes on to suggest that Spinoza helps us,

to move away from dualistic understandings of sexual difference (sex/gender) and towards understanding differences as constituted through relatively stable but dynamic networks of relational powers, capacities and affects. Spinoza's immanent and monistic theory of being . . . allows one to theorize the interconnections between sexed bodies and other body complexes, such as the body politic or other institutional assemblages (the law, for example). It is only within these complex assemblages that sexed bodies are produced as socially and politically meaningful bodies . . . Since Spinoza maintains that there can be no causal relation between mind and body (since both are modifications of the attributes of a single substance, or nature), sex, in some sense, must be gender, though 'expressed' or made manifest through the attribute of extension rather than thought. This amounts to saying that sex is a particular extensive 'organization' of the material powers and capacities of a body, whereas gender would amount to the affective powers and affects of such a body. (149)

Such an understanding renders both 'sex' and 'gender' dynamic, both of them being conceived as 'complex fields of interconnecting powers and affects' (149).

The Spinozo-Deleuzian conception of bodies, assemblages, the role of affects and the imagination gives rise to a more adequate way of thinking sex and gender, one which is more in keeping with recent technological developments, whereby transitioning from one sex to another has become feasible, and the concepts of sex and gender are construed as fluid and malleable, as part of a nexus that is just one aspect of complex entities and relations. At the same time, it provides a useful way of thinking about how body images, or corporeal schema, are always already derivative of, although not reducible to, what Benedict Anderson has called 'imagined communities' (1991), powerful, shared, normative fictions or myths that dictate sometimes racialized national imaginaries. Stylized, gendered imaginaries also inform our psychic, habituated modes of life, encouraging us, for example, to measure ourselves against idealized images of femininity, and to find ourselves wanting. One can see how such normative fictions illuminate practices such as anorexia nervosa and bulimia. At the same time it is necessary to attend to the specific dynamic of such practices, without resorting to explaining eating disorders as if they were simply a result of imbibing cultural ideals of thinness (see Mclane, 2003).

In order to see how Deleuze, particularly in his reading of Spinoza, can provide resources for feminist theory, we will need to familiarize ourselves, albeit in a limited fashion, with a few details of Deleuze's approach. In particular, Deleuze takes up Spinoza, who, in moving beyond Descartes' mind–body dualism, introduces a philosophy in which he not only appeals to the body, rather than the mind, as the model for philosophers (see Deleuze 1988, 17), but also accords a more privileged role to affects than Descartes – whose attachment to rationality is well known. The importance of the body and affects – typically denigrated by a masculine-identified tradition – has of course provided feminist theory with resources for thinking that often seem to have escaped the dominant philosophical tradition. Spinoza proves to be the exception to the tradition in this regard; Deleuze's return to Spinoza has helped bring this to light, and in doing so has proved to be a valuable impetus for feminist philosophers, from Braidotti to Gatens. In *Metamorphoses*, adopting a Deleuzian idiom, Braidotti suggests that 'the point is not to know who we are, but rather, what, at last, we want to become . . . Or, as Laurie Anderson put it wittily: nowadays moods are more important than modes of being' (2002, 2).

To say that Spinoza takes the body, rather than the mind, as his model, should not be taken to indicate that he merely reverses the Cartesian position. If Descartes defines humans as essentially thinking, rather than extended, bodily, substances, 'Spinoza rejects any superiority of the mind over the body . . . not in order to establish a superiority of the body over the mind, which would be no more intelligible than the converse' (Deleuze 1988, 18; see also Mullarkey 1997, 447). As Gatens and Lloyd say, 'For Spinoza, minds and bodies are united not in causal interactions but in the relations of ideas to their objects' (1999, 1). At stake for Deleuze is Spinoza's overturning of the assumption that consciousness dominates the passions, and in doing so founds a morality that is ostensibly based upon the privilege of reason. Rather, according to Spinoza's parallelism, 'the body surpasses the knowledge we have of it, *and . . . thought likewise surpasses the knowledge that we have of it*' (Deleuze 1988, 18). Philosophy, then, according to Deleuze, is neither a matter of consciousness dominating the passions – a view that would issue in a moralism that Deleuze, following Nietzsche, condemns – nor is it a matter of conscious reflection, as in the meditative model adopted by Descartes, and adapted by phenomenology, which assumes that philosophical method is a matter of rendering more rigorous that which we always already do as a matter of course.

Whether it is a question of Heidegger's move from the pre-ontological to the ontological 'understanding of Being' (see Deleuze 1994, 129) or Descartes' extrapolation of a philosophical method, Deleuze is critical of the idea that the impulse of philosophy lies in rendering explicit that which is already implicit. Thus 'conceptual philosophical thought has as its implicit presupposition a pre-philosophical and natural Image of thought, borrowed from the pure element of common sense' (Deleuze 1994, 131). Since he starts from the premise that everybody already knows what it is to think, all Descartes has to do is render what we all already (supposedly) do more rigorous, by disciplining thought. 'It is because everybody naturally thinks, that everybody is supposed to know implicitly what it means to think' (131). The idea that thought is a 'natural capacity' with which we are all endowed, and that it is allied to, or has 'an affinity' (131) with truth is not one that Deleuze accepts. In fact, for him, 'men think rarely, and more often under the impulse of a shock than the excitement of a taste for thinking' (132). 'Something in the world forces us to think. This something is an object not of recognition but of a fundamental *encounter*' (139). What we encounter 'may be grasped in a range of affective tones: wonder, love, hatred, suffering . . . The object of encounter . . . gives rise to sensibility' (139). Whereas Descartes' procedure of radical doubt, elevated to a method for philosophy, consists of systematically discarding the contingent and the accidental, in order to preserve the necessary and the essential, for Deleuze, it is precisely the 'involuntary,' 'illegitimate,' 'fortuitous' (139) and even the 'monstrous' (1995, 6) that should be celebrated. It is 'strangeness' or 'enmity' that awakens us to thought (1994, 139). In concluding that the only thing he can be certain of is '*I think therefore I am*' (cogito ergo sum) (Descartes 1979, 101), Descartes appeals to a model of recognition, and in doing so, he privileges harmony. He seeks agreement among all the faculties, grounded in the unity of his concept of the self.

As Deleuze says: 'The form of recognition has never sanctioned anything but the recognizable and the recognized; form will never inspire anything but conformities' (1994, 134). When the Declaration of Human Rights was interpreted in such a way as to fail to extend equality to slaves, or to grant that they were as civilized as those who wielded power over them, what was at stake was a failure to recognize them as fully human. In order to qualify as human, it would seem, one had to be seen to imitate, or approximate to, the masters. The difference in skin color thereby became indicative of the failure of African-American slaves to represent an allegedly ideal humanity, embodied by whites, who took themselves to be the incarnation of true humanity. The model of representation and truth at work here is under attack by Deleuze, for whom Nietzsche's critique, not of 'false claims to truth but truth in itself and as an ideal' is pertinent (Deleuze 1983, 95). To will the truth is to oppose the world with 'another world' (96) – a world beyond this world, a world of eternal truth. To do so is to want 'life to repudiate itself and to turn against itself' (96).

> The one who repudiates life is also the one who wants a diminished life, the conversation of *his* type and moreover its power and triumph, the triumph and contagion of reactive forces. At this point reactive forces discover the disturbing ally that leads them to victory: nihilism, the will to nothingness [see Nietzsche, 1989]. The will to nothingness which can only bear life in its reactive form. The will to nothingness is the one that used reactive forces as a way of ensuring that life *must* contradict, deny and annihilate itself. (96–7)

To get back to Descartes, take the example of wax, by which Descartes seeks to show that the very thing that we might have been tempted to rely upon, namely the evidence of the senses, must in fact be discounted as unreliable. Unlit, the wax of a candle is hard, cylindrical, and solid in colour; yet if I light it, its properties change: the same candle becomes soft, its volume expands, and it becomes translucent. How, then, can I rely on the evidence of my senses, on what my sight, touch, smell, hearing, and taste tell me? The knowledge that it is the same candle, despite its changes, must come from elsewhere. My ability to recognize that the identity of the candle has not changed, appearances notwithstanding, derives from the agreement among the various faculties, based on the 'unity of a thinking subject' which provides the 'ground' of 'the form of identity' (Deleuze 1994, 133). 'Recognition thus relies upon a ground in the unity of a thinking subject, of which all the other faculties must be modalities. This is the meaning of the Cogito as a beginning' (133). Hence, 'Recognition may be defined by the harmonious exercise of all the faculties upon a supposed same object: the same object may be seen, touched, remembered, imagined or conceived . . . As Descartes says of the piece of wax: "It is of course the same wax which I see, which I touch, which I picture in my imagination, in short the same wax which I thought it to be from the start" ' (Deleuze 1994, 133; Descartes 1979, 155 [alternative translation]). In the process of thereby establishing the priority of thinking over the senses, Descartes runs together the different functions of the faculties, superimposing on them a unity that ignores their divergence.

For Deleuze, philosophy goes wrong when it assumes that thinking, being and self are concepts that somehow are already known in advance or that, as Deleuze puts it, 'Everybody knows' (1994, 130). Given the importance of Spinoza for Deleuze's thinking, and given that it 'is more likely' for 'Writers, poets, musicians, filmmakers – painters too, even chance readers' to 'find that they are Spinozists . . . than for professional philosophers' (1988, 129) perhaps it is not accidental that 'Everybody knows' is a refrain from one of best songs written by poet and musician Leonard Cohen! After all, Deleuze privileges Anglo-American literature over French, because the French are too caught up in history. 'They do not know how to become' (Deleuze and Parnet 2002, 37). By contrast, 'American literature operates according to geographical lines: the flight towards the West . . . The becoming is geographical' (37). Deleuze and Guattari are attentive to the metaphors at use in philosophical systems, which they weigh carefully, since such metaphors have a good deal of impact on what they call the 'image of thought.' As Patton says: 'Against the arborescent image which has been prevalent in the history of philosophy, they propose a rhizomatic image of thought in which concepts are never stable but in a state of constant flux as they are modified or transformed in the passage from one problem to the next' (2000, 16–17). Structuralism is a 'system of points and positions, which operates by cuts which are supposedly significant instead of proceeding by thrusts and crackings. It warps the lines of flight instead of following them and tracing them and extending them in a social field' (Deleuze and Parnet 2002, 37). The French 'are too fond of roots, trees, the survey, the points of arborescence, the properties' (Deleuze and Parnet 2002, 37). Deleuze elevates the image of the 'rhizome' over that of 'tree' (1994, xvii; see Patton 2000, 17). Rhizomatic thinking, as opposed to the arborescent, or majoritarian schema, as Braidotti puts it, 'encourages each subject to empower him- or herself as a multiplicity and among multiple axes' (2002, 74–5). The rhizome model 'operates as an immanent process' and 'unlike trees or their roots, the rhizome connects any point to any other point' and 'is made only of lines'; it is 'antigenealogy. It is a short-term memory' which 'operates by variation, expansion, conquest, capture, offshoots . . . the rhizome pertains to a map that must be produced, constructed' (Deleuze and Guattari 1988, 20–1).

Deleuze draws his images from geography, from the natural elements, from landscapes, and from animality. At the same time, he draws on the arts, following up an injunction of Spinoza, who 'teaches the philosopher how to become a nonphilosopher' (1988, 130). Spinoza's *Ethics* (1955) is characterized by Deleuze as a 'riverbook' (1997, 151). As a 'discourse of the concept' it appears as 'a long, tranquil, and powerful river' (145). Yet at the same time the *Ethics* is 'a book of fire' (151). 'It is like a broken chain, discontinuous, subterranean, volcanic, which at irregular intervals comes to interrupt the chain of demonstrative elements, the great and continuous fluvial chain' (146). Yet another image is applied to book V of the *Ethics*, 'an aerial book of light' (151), so that there are not one but three 'ethics' – that of the sign, that of the concept and that of essence, constituting 'the same world,' connected by 'bridges' (151). Along with 'zones,' 'movable bridges' are 'the joints of a concept,' the 'junctures, or detours' (Deleuze and Guattari 1994, 20; 22). Again, the *Ethics* is a 'musical composition' (1988, 126). If Spinoza's *Ethics* is a river – or fire, or light, or music, depending on which aspect one emphasizes, concepts are 'like multiple waves' and a plane of immanence is a 'single wave,' or it is like a 'desert' (Deleuze and Guattari, 1994, 36). Notions such as becoming-animal also pervade Deleuze's work. 'What if', asks Braidotti, 'by comparison with the know-how of animals, conscious self-representation were blighted by narcissistic delusions and consequently blinded by its own aspirations to self-transparency?' (2002, 136). Lorraine makes a point of distinguishing becoming-animal and from imitating animals. 'True becoming-animal engages the subject at the limits of the corporeal and conceptual logics already formed and so brings on the destabilization of conscious awareness that forces the subject to a genuinely creative response' (1999, 181–2).

Deleuze and Guattari also famously discuss 'becoming-woman' (1988, 275–6). Pelagia Goulimari suggests that we read their descriptions of 'becoming-woman' along with their claim that 'all becomings begin with and pass through becoming-woman' (1988, 277). They thus:

> recognize feminism's success in opening the way to the desire of becoming other, that is, other than one's 'self,' other than a branch on the tree of Man, other than a subordinate referent of Majority Rule. Second, these descriptions serve to remind us of feminism's historic responsibility to keep this way open to its own and other minoritarian movements, to its own and other subordinate points, so that 'woman' sheds its quality of being a universal referent and becomes a multiplicity of collective reference-machines and machines of expression. (1999, 103)

Since becoming-animal and becoming-woman, discussed in chapter ten of *A Thousand Plateaus*, are themes that have been pursued at length, and perhaps more in-depth than other Deleuzian themes, rather than duplicating these discussions, I refer the reader to the work of those who have already treated it, such as Braidotti (2002), Lorraine (1999), Olkowski (2000), Conley (2000), and Flieger (2000).

All concepts have different components: 'there is no simple concept' (Deleuze and Guattari 1994, 19). Descartes' cogito, 'I think therefore I am' has three components: 'doubting, thinking, and being' (24). These components are 'simple *variations*' (20). The 'I' functions as a point of condensation (see 20). That Deleuze is critical of the authority of psychoanalysis does not entail his utter repudiation of it. On the contrary, the influence of psychoanalysis is evident on his thinking. It is doubtful, for example, that Deleuze would have used the term 'condensation' (see 20–1) in the way that he does, were it not for the privilege that psychoanalysis has accorded the term. This is no aberration, given that 'every concept always has a history' and that 'In any concept there are usually bits or components that come from other concepts' (18).

'I am a thinking being' closes the concept of the self, as a 'fragmentary totality' (26). Concepts are joined by bridges. In Descartes' *Meditations*, the 'bridge' from 'the concept of self to the concept of God' (26) is Descartes' claim that one of the ideas that I have is that of God, and the very concept of God necessarily implies the idea of infinity: 'among my ideas is the idea of infinity' (26). Like 'the concept of the self,' 'the concept of God' also has three components – the three proofs for the existence of God. In turn, the third, ontological proof of God constitutes a bridge to another concept, that of extension. Thus Descartes constructs a kind of 'dry-stone wall,' held together with 'diverging lines' (23). Concepts 'pass back and forth' between their components, which are 'inseparable' from one another: this is what gives concepts their 'consistency' (23).

Kant's cogito 'renders doubt useless' (31) and challenges Descartes' concept of the cogito for eliminating time from the concept of the self. In doing so, Kant creates a new concept of the cogito. The Kantian concept has four, not three components, one of which is time, but in introducing time into the concept of the self, Kant also changes the concept of time. Time is no longer a 'form of anteriority,' as it had been for Plato, nor a 'simple mode of succession referring to continuous creation,' as it had been for Descartes; it now becomes a 'form of interiority' (32). Time now becomes a component of the cogito, where Descartes had expelled it, or 'repressed' it (31). The cogito is reborn – it is defined by a new plane, and by a new problem. The Cartesian plane on which the cogito occurs was to challenge any explicit objective presupposition (see 26), and the problem to which the cogito answered was: 'beginning with what concept can truth as absolutely pure subjective certainty be determined?' (26–7). Kant's plane is the 'transcendental' (31), but he remains caught up in the dogmatic image of thought.

One could continue tracing how concepts are revived by philosophers, who rejuvenate them, but in the process also challenge the philosophers who originally signed them – indeed, Deleuze and Guattari encourage the introduction of new examples (see 19). Levinas, for example, returns to a Cartesian conception of time in his privileging of instantaneity and discontinuity, and his emphasis of the novelty that each new instant introduces into time, which is now conceived as breaking up, as interrupted, with each new instant, and falling back into itself – a continuous discontinuity. If in one way Levinas breathes new life into Descartes' idea of time, as that which is recreated at each moment, in another way, he breathes new life into Kant's idea of the subject, who, as Deleuze and Guattari put it 'becomes an other' (32). For Levinas, it is the Other, not the I that is at the center of the world. The philosopher's world is no longer egocentric. While for Kant the subject becomes an other to itself through the feat of representation, as 'necessarily representing its own thinking activity to itself as an Other (Autrui)' (32), for Levinas time itself comes from the other (see Levinas 1987), and as such it is the Other, not God (as it is for Descartes), who renews the subject at every instant. The Other recreates me, or gives me new birth: the Other, to whom I am infinitely responsible, is the one that makes me other to myself, not my own capacity for representing myself to myself (as it is for Kant). Descartes' cogito is therefore not just displaced by Levinas, by way of a Kantian detour that itself becomes revitalized, it is evicted from the system altogether. The subject is no longer centered on the 'I think,' nor on being, nor on doubt, but is radically decentered by the alterity of the other. It is no longer a question of 'I think therefore I am,' it is rather that I discover myself as having already been in relation to the Other, and as such responsible since time immemorial. Levinas's concept of alterity, one might say, together with its components – responsibility, infinity, and the fecundity of time – defines the subject as oriented otherwise than towards being. One could fill in the details of this history, by showing how Bergsonian duration and Heideggerian Being are taken up and rethought in Levinas's philosophy, and themselves become stages on the itinerary undertaken by the history of concepts on their way from Descartes to the twentieth century. Or one could track an alternative history, perhaps through Hegel and Rosenzweig – but the point should be clear. Concepts are determined anew by the problems for which they are called into being to answer. As these problems shift, so too are new concepts called into being, such that one component falls out of consideration in order to make way for another – and in the process, the concept is reborn.

I said earlier that there is a sense in which Deleuze writes difference back into the canon: 'there is no true beginning in philosophy, or rather that the true philosophical beginning, Difference, is in-itself already Repetition' (1994, 129). In the case of Descartes, Deleuze locates his effacing of difference in his grounding of the faculties in the cogito as the seat of unity, as if conceiving, judging, imagining, remembering, and perceiving were all merely variations of thought, or the thinking subject. Deleuze says: 'The "I think" is the most general principle of representation' (138). It is 'source . . . of the unity of all th[e] faculties: I conceive, I judge, I imagine, I remember and I perceive – as though these were the four branches of the Cogito. On precisely these branches, difference is crucified' (138).

Having gained at least a brief insight into Deleuze's Spinozistic view, let's consolidate its pertinence for feminist concerns by returning to Gatens, who argues that its anti-dualistic, anti-juridical, and anti-humanist perspective provides us with a valuable lesson. Rather than the Hobbesian view of law and order, which is based on a dualist ontology, and assumes that the function of political order consists of overseeing human affects and dispositions, Deleuze resists, along with Spinoza, the separation of two distinct planes that this model implies. For Hobbes, culture and nature belong to two different orders, and since human beings tend to be lawless, the relations between them tending to degenerate into a war of all against all, they are in need of government. Hence the need to procure a social contract, the norms of which must be imposed from a sovereign who acts from above, and is sanctioned by God, as transcendent. Spinoza, on the contrary, does not conceive of nature as separate from transcendent norms that come from elsewhere. He resists the dualistic view of nature vs culture or body vs mind. Although Deleuze and Guattari distinguish a plane of transcendence from a plane of immanence, they also maintain that 'there is no dualism between the two planes of transcendent organization and immanent consistence . . . We do not speak of a dualism between two kinds of "things," but of a multiplicity of dimensions, of lines and directions in the heart of an assemblage' (Deleuze and Parnet 2002, 132–3). The distinction between molar and molecular provides two different viewpoints: a transcendent viewpoint – the one followed by Hobbes, when he thinks it is necessary to invoke political order from above, or by psychoanalysis, when it imposes the Oedipal triangle as the orchestrator of the drives, or operates according to the fixed binary opposition man/woman. As Gatens says: 'The plane of transcendence attempts to *organize* the plane of nature into fixed molar forms' (2000, 61), defined by genus and species (man/woman, human/animal), according to their functions. The plane of immanence (the second viewpoint), on the other hand, is one of experimentation; it is dynamic, not fixed. It is mobile or molecular. 'Each thing is implicated in a ceaseless process of *becoming* something else' (Gatens 2000, 61)

Spinoza's monism consists of the view that there is only one substance, which he calls God, and that this substance is nothing other than nature itself, conceived immanently. For Spinoza, God is, as Gatens says, 'the creative and entirely immanent power of active nature . . . there is only one immanent substance, and human being is a mode of the attributes of nature – thought and extension. Knowledge or the power of thought, is our most powerful affect, and everything that exists strives to persevere in its being' (2000, 60). On Spinoza's view, human bodies are not particularly privileged over other bodies: 'a body can be anything; it can be an animal, a body of sounds, a mind or an idea; it can be a linguistic corpus, a social body, a collectivity' (Deleuze 1988, 127). Human freedom is essentially a matter of selecting encounters that promote joyful rather than sad affects. This facilitates a rethinking of sex and gender such that sex, gender, class, and race are 'molecular combinations' (Gatens 2000, 65). Rather than construing reason as disembodied, and bodies as essentially passive, the 'human being is conceived as part of a dynamic and interconnected whole' (60–1), and the 'the body is in constant interchange with its environment. Spinoza understands the body as a nexus of variable interconnections, a multiplicity.' 'For Spinoza, body and mind necessarily suffer or act in concert' (61).

The idea that bodies – whether physical or institutional – are complex wholes, intersected with different forces, and that the concepts of sex and gender should be thought of at the level of the molecular, and not merely in terms of the molar, is a fertile one for feminist theory. It allows us to do away with the privileging of sexual difference over other differences, and it allows us to situate feminist theory fairly and squarely in the realm of political discourse, where it should be – not cut off in some ethereal, academic realm of gender studies. Race, class, ethnicity, religion, age, sexuality, are different facets or aspects of an institutional body, for example, which converge or coalesce at certain points, which crystallize in certain bodies, at certain historical moments or which come to embody certain configurations of power. At a particular historical and political juncture, a number of forces converge to represent bodies in particular ways. Active, youthful bodies with darker skin, for example, bodies that are raced and masculinized in certain ways, according to the power regimes that organize airport security, are liable to be organized into a certain molar type: those likely to be regarded with more suspicion than other bodies by security guards. When the political and affective powers (a singular and peculiar mixture of domination, paranoia, and fear) that produce such suspicion wane, or take on new contours, different bodies will be regarded with suspicion. The organizing principle will become something else – more or less dictatorial, more or less bound up with the American war on Iraq, and the subsequent terrorist attacks suffered in the rest of the world. The Bush administration was content for a long while to marginalize the concerns Cindy Sheehan brought to public attention, painting a picture of her as a distraught, emotional, out of control mother, whose pain was understandable but irrational. When public opinion polls began to shift, registering that Sheehan's objections to the war, far from constituting the marginalized, offbeat, sentimental ravings of a bitter woman, in fact represented the majority opinion, it became harder to diminish and denigrate her views as those of an out of control, unpatriotic female. She became more of a threat. Clearly, the manipulation of gender stereotypes in this case played into how the administration chose to deal with Sheehan's objections to the war.

Feminist theorists have used Deleuze and Guattari's experimental and affirmative philosophy to produce new and innovative readings of philosophers such as Beauvoir (see Secomb 1999). It is worth noting also, that a number of feminist theorists have drawn compelling parallels between the work of Irigaray and Deleuze, including Braidotti (1991; 1994; 2000) Lorraine (1999), and Olkowski (2000). The challenge that Deleuze and Guattari present to the traditional way in which the history of philosophy has functioned has provided feminism with a breath of fresh air. Deleuze comments that Spinoza, 'more than any other gave me a feeling of a gust of air from behind' (Deleuze and Parnet 2002, 15). One might say the same about the relationship between Deleuze and Guattari and feminist theory, insofar as their philosophical contributions have inspired a good number of the most original and interesting feminist theorists, among them Gatens and Braidotti.

CHAPTER 7

CONCLUDING REFLECTIONS

We have seen that feminist theory opposed the way in which the concept of 'sex' functions as a legitimating truth that normatively constrains gender. Operating as a stable ground, foundation, or origin, biological sex is taken as a natural, causal, and moral explanation for how women should act, appear, and be. Theories that construct biological sex as a foundational premise involve several assumptions. First, they divide sexuality into two and only two, mutually exclusive categories or sexes: male and female. Second, they attribute exclusively heteronormative sexual aims to each sex. Third, they tend to conflate the capacity for reproduction with a moral argument about the purpose of sexual activity – unless sex is undertaken by a male and a female for reproductive purposes, it is considered suspect. It is not hard to discern the Christian fundamentalist ethic, in which Adam and Eve are the role models, informing such a framework.

While it appears to be the case that feminists departed from traditional notions that sex precedes gender, Delphy and others show that in fact this assumption was often left in place, and that it needs to be questioned. By leaving in place the fundamental priority of sex, even while attempting to dismantle it, feminism still appears to be governed by that which it opposes, and in this sense it remains reactive. Delphy argues that the assumption that sex precedes gender functions as an unexamined presupposition not only in traditional, conservative arguments, but also in many feminist arguments. This assumption is one that needs to be questioned, rather than confirmed. While feminist arguments that privilege gender over sex seek to question the traditional privileging of sex over gender, they end up by leaving the precedence of sex over gender in place, by reaffirming it. Sex functions as the dominant, primary, or foundational term of a hierarchy, in which gender functions as the subordinate, derivative, or supplementary term. As supplementary, gender appears to be marginal or secondary to the fundamental ground of sex, but in fact it turns out to generate its meaning. Far from being causally determined by 'sex,' where sex precedes and produces gender, normative, stereotypical feminine ways of behaving and being (passivity, weakness, inferiority, indecision) turn out to be cultural traits that find their way into the discursive construction of 'biology.' Educational accounts of procreation are rife with rhetoric that enforces the stereotypes that align men with virility, courage, bravery, strength, and adventuresome spirits, while women are relegated to the receptive, secondary role of passive and inactive containers. While the wiry sperm make their way along the dark, mysterious channels of female anatomy, towards the uterus, thwarted at every turn by the dangers that await them, the ova lie recumbent, passive and ready to be penetrated. Millions of sperm perish along the way, but should a single sperm succeed in its daring mission, should it conquer the barricades that sometimes prove to be insurmountable, entering the fortress of an ovum, fertilization succeeds, and the miracle of procreation begins! Cut to the happy, smiling face of a newborn baby – and forget the extremely active exertion and pain of pregnancy and labor.

Once the rhetorical basis of the very accounts of ostensibly biological processes is exposed, it becomes clear that sex is always already gendered – that the 'natural' ground of sex is in fact the constructed projection of culturally specific, hegemonic ideas about gender. Theories of sexuality are promulgated by those whose political interests set the theoretical agenda. Sex is not a given, but our ideas of what it should be are constructed by juridical, medical, religious, and political discourses that overlap and compete with one another for legitimate definitions. If an infant is born with sexual organs that make its gender ambiguous, surgical intervention is called for in order to bring it into line with normative categories. As Scott puts it, the question is 'how, in what specific contexts, among which specific communities of people, and by what textual and social processes has meaning been acquired? . . . How do meanings change? How have some meanings emerged as normative and others have been eclipsed or disappeared? What do these processes reveal about how power is constituted and operates?' (1998, 35). The destabilization of normative distinctions that have protected the interests of the powerful, at the cost of those who have traditionally lacked power, provides an example of the importance of redefining apparently timeless truths. The slogan 'the personal is the political' has played an important part in defining the movement of feminism. We are reminded by bell hooks that to refuse to conceive of politics as a realm that is autonomous and rigidly separate from the personal is not merely a matter of individual women expressing the ways in which they have been victimized, but rather a question of developing systemic, political critiques of how consciousness can be colonized. Out of such critique, political change can ensue. Rape is a case in point.

With the help of feminist analyses, a rape victim can begin to understand her trauma not solely in terms of the individual and personal suffering that it has caused her, but also to develop a political analysis of her situation, focusing on the structural conditions that foster rape as a violent crime against women. By developing an understanding of rape in the context of a shared experience with other victims of rape, and by construing rape as something that is condoned by the practices of a patriarchal society, the tendency of a rape victim to blame themselves for what has happened, as if the event could have been averted if only she had not worn 'provocative' clothing or acted as if she were 'available' (i.e. a self-determining free agent) can be alleviated. The act of telling one's story can, in and of itself, be a way of re-positioning oneself in relation to a trauma. Rape induces shame and humiliation. Finding the strength and resources to communicate one's experience to others can play a part in overcoming the trauma of rape, and at the same time can help to establish a shared community, from which other women, both victims of rape and potential victims of rape, can gather insight. The importance of breaking the silence about rape lies not only in its potential to alleviate the private suffering of rape victims, but also in the correction of the historical record, and in the potential for transforming the ways in which people think about rape. Breaking the silence can foster communities of individuals who have suffered similar experiences, and out of those communities can emerge demands for change, which not only enable women who have been victims of rape, but also help to prevent future rapes, by raising awareness about the nature and preventability of rape.

By successfully challenging the implicit understanding of wives as the property of husbands, feminists demanded legal changes prohibiting the fact of being married to a woman from constituting a legitimate defense against rape. Against the pernicious idea that rape is due to an uncontrollable, 'biological' urge in the face of which men find themselves helpless, feminists have insisted that there is no sense in which rape is inevitable. Using the example of the Mir space station, in which one woman was on board in a confined space with men for a period of several months, Margaret Setz shows that rape occurs with impunity only when it is legitimated. 'When it is not in the political interests of a government or of its military arm, then rape stops' (2001, 94). Building on the work of Susan Brownmiller (1975), feminists have redefined rape, so that it is no longer understood as an aggressive form of sexuality, but rather an act of violence that is expressed sexually. Feminists have also clarified that the 'past sexual history' of women is irrelevant to their rape. Prostitutes are raped too. The clothes that a woman happens to be wearing, whether or not she is inebriated, whether or not she is a virgin – none of these factors are relevant in determining whether or not a rape has taken place. They do not, and should not be taken to indicate, that 'she was asking for it.' What is relevant is whether or not she said 'no,' whether or not she resisted, whether or not she was forced, in Susan Brownmiller's words, 'against her will.' 'No' means no, as feminists have reiterated time and again. The equally important corollary of this is that 'yes' means yes, that sex between two consenting adults should not be portrayed as demeaning to either party.

Setz argues that Asian feminists have led the way in demanding that their governments face up to their implication in rape, by organizing conferences, demonstrations, and publications in which the stories of those who have been victims of wartime rape come to light. By the same token, they have demonstrated an exemplary relationship between academic feminism and activism, showing the need for feminism in the classroom to translate into positive political changes on the ground. Telling their stories enables rape victims to transform their status as victims to one of overcoming trauma. It makes visible stories and events that the official versions of history, told from the perspective of the vanquishers, often overlooks. Documenting the history of rape in wartime provides evidence on the basis of which demands for accountability on the part of those who have committed or condoned rape can be launched.

Among the practical pay-offs of feminist analyses we can count the shift of the definition of rape as understood in the context of the Geneva Convention, as analyzed by Setz. Previously understood as a crime against honor, rape is now defined as a crime against humanity. As a result of this challenge, prosecution of rape became possible for the first time. In 1996, eight Bosnian Serb military and police officials were indicted by the United Nations International Criminal Tribunal of the Hague for the war crime of rape. At the same time, Setz points out, feminists have encouraged an analysis of rape in wartime which focuses on 'the culture, laws, military systems, and governments' (2001, 93) that legitimate it, rather than focusing solely on the individuals who committed the crimes. Furthermore, as a result of feminist work on rape, new forms of therapy have been developed for those recovering from the trauma of rape. Kelly Oliver has developed the importance of witnessing in other contexts (see Oliver 2001).

Such is the complexity of lived experience that abstract, philosophical, and largely reflective attempts to grasp its contours can often obscure, overlook, or distort important facets. While concepts help to bring clarity and order to our reflections, they can, at times, obfuscate the very texture of life they are intended to clarify. Essays and narratives are sometimes more successful in capturing the ebb and flow of life – what Henri Bergson called *la durée* (duration). As such they can illuminate philosophy. By way of concluding this discussion, I draw on a text that explores in a literary way some of the questions that feminist philosophers have explored conceptually. Deleuze and Guattari distinguish between art and philosophy by suggesting that if philosophy creates new concepts, 'Art thinks no less than philosophy, but it thinks through affects and percepts' (1994, 66), whereas the 'concept belongs to philosophy and only to philosophy' (34). Art, according to Deleuze, 'can grasp events' (1995, 160). Art, philosophy and science should be seen as 'separate melodic lines in constant interplay with one another' (125). To borrow the words of Tamsin Lorraine's essay on Derrida and Deleuze, 'To be worthy of an event is to respond to the generating force of sense as a dynamic and always unpredictable force of becoming' (2003, 39). In a profound and moving narrative of a vacation she took in the Bahamas, June Jordan demonstrates the complexity of relations between race, class, and gender, revealing that these concepts operate in ways that are far from automatic. It is not who you are, not your identity, that counts, but rather what you know, what you have learned, and what you are prepared to do about it that forges political and ethical connections between people. Such connections can grow out of similar experiences, or they can grow out of dissimilar experiences. Jordan questions the legitimacy of history that passes for mainstream, whether it is the history of the Bahamas told by the plastic pages of the welcoming package in the hotel room of The Sheraton British Colonial that begins in 1492 with Christopher Columbus, thereby ignoring the black people of the Bahamas, or the history represented by university syllabi. Like the victims of wartime sexual violence, the characters who people Jordan's essays typically do not make it into this history. They have 'neither killed nor conquered anyone.' They are 'the ones who wash and who feed and who teach and who diligently decorate straw hats and bags with all of their historically unrequired [*sic*] love: the women' (Jordan 2003, 217).

Among them also numbers the smiling black middle-aged man who looks out at the tourists from an advertising photograph, in which he 'is so delighted to serve you' a drink that, fully clothed, 'he will wade into the water to bring you Banana Daquiris . . . and he will do it with a smile' (211). Such people are represented as 'servile ancillar[ies] to the pleasures of the rich' (212). They are the 'frequently toothless Black women' who 'argue . . . the price of hand-woven goods at the local straw market' (212) with tourists on vacation. They are the anonymous, unseen hotel maids who clean hotel rooms, like 'Olive' (213), whom Jordan is invited to rate on a scale from excellent to poor.

So long as we imagine that the simple fact of race, gender, or class establishes a connection between you and someone who shares the same race, gender, or class, we are misled. Jordan might share the same gender as the woman sitting on the street who wants to sell her a handwoven basket, she might share the same gender as Olive, but her class and American privilege separates her life experience from that of Olive. Jordan might have the same skin color as the man who wades, fully clothed, into the sea to serve tourists like her Daquiris. Yet a chasm separates them. Race, gender, and class do not forge automatic connections between people. As Jordan points out, 'the ultimate connection cannot be the enemy' (219). This is what Nietzsche means when he points to the limitations of reactive thinking, advocating instead active, affirmative, productive relations. For feminists to remain consumed with the patriarchal enemy is to allow ourselves to be defined by an oppositional politics. For women to play the 'blame men' card is to remain caught up in *ressentiment*, rather than creatively forging new relations, that do not fall into the mold of what Nietzsche calls the slave morality (see 1968, 31–2). In Jordan's words,

> I am reaching for the words to describe the difference between a common identity that has been imposed and the individual identity any one of us will choose, once she gains that chance.
> That difference is the one that keeps us stupid in the face of new, specific information about somebody else with whom we are supposed to have a connection because a third party, hostile to both of us, has worked it so that the two of us, like it or not, share a common enemy. *What happens beyond the idea of that enemy and beyond the consequences of that enemy?* (2003, 219)

Jordan's answer to this question comes in the form of a narrative, one that features the connection that is formed between two students, after they had both fled the racism of their respective countries. Cathy, a young Irish woman finds a way of befriending Sokutu, a South African woman who is being beaten by her alcoholic husband. Through becoming her friend, and gaining her trust, Cathy is able to help her. What Cathy does is to reach out her hands to Sokutu, and tell her she understands about alcoholism, that her father was a violent alcoholic. She helps her find a safe place to stay, and she says, 'I want to be your friend.' Jordan's observation is that 'it was not who they were but what they both know and what they were both preparing to do about what they know that was going to make them both free at last' (222).

Under another name, what Jordan is objecting to is a naïve version of identity politics. The important point is that we learn to overcome the biographical and historical factors that keep us apart from one another, or set us against one another, so that we can focus on how we can learn from our experiences in ways that enable us to be supportive, sustaining, and strong for one another, rather than allowing our differences to be divisive, antagonistic, and full of resentment. We must learn to build new communities across difference, which will sometimes mean leaving our comfort zones and taking risks. It will mean opening ourselves up to criticism and misunderstanding, it will mean making mistakes and being embarrassed, it will mean learning new ways of doing things, sometimes feeling stupid, and getting things wrong. It will mean learning about ourselves, revising our ideas, and being ready, able, and willing to learn from others whose experiences have been very different from ours, and sometimes might have been negatively impacted by the privileges that we have been able to unreflectively assume. It will mean taking risks.

Feminist analyses, which, I would argue, are important in and of themselves, in the sense that conceptual clarity about political and social movements is usually helpful – even if its rigidity can sometimes stand in the way of political progress on the ground – have also resulted in some important transformations in the realm of praxis. I would add that political initiatives, in their turn, have fed into, have been taken up by, and have altered the shape of feminist theory. The relationship between practice and theory is perhaps less dialectical than mutually constitutive. Each feeds into the other, so that their relationship is one in which concrete experience and political practice informs theory, while theory, for its part, helps to guide or dictate political action. Yet neither theory nor practice is autonomous or complete in and of themselves, neither is left untouched by their encounter with one another, and it is not always clear how one is indebted to the other until after such encounters. Their relationship is more nebulous, and the exchange that takes place between them less determinate. Each will be influenced by the other, in ways that will not always be easy to cash out: the relationship is not one in which theory cancels out or supersedes practice, or vice versa, but rather one in which practice will flow into, or disrupt, theory and theory will shape, or contest, practice.

With the achievement of certain feminist ends, feminism itself becomes transformed into a new kind of struggle, one that can assume as its historical ground a set of accomplishments on which it can stand and build (see Kristeva 1986). Once the economic, legal, and political parity of women with men had been achieved, for instance – at least at the theoretical level (in substantive terms, we still have a good way to go) – feminism is both free to, and has an obligation to, reconstitute itself. It must reflect on its successes (agreement that legally women must be remunerated with equal pay for equal work, equal voting rights, equal opportunity in education and sports, for example), and on the basis of its historical development, on the basis of what it has become, it must reformulate its goals. This task of reformulation must be a continual process. One way in which feminism has had to rethink its fundamental tenets is by becoming more inclusive. Part of this effort resides in the capacity of feminist thinking to incorporate international points of view, to produce theory that is informed by its nature as a transnational movement. Another obligation feminism has is to be answerable to the challenges with which transgendered identity presents it. A third area that feminism must confront is the need to formulate new models for the kind of thinking demanded by a movement that seeks to avoid exclusivity. I have suggested that the model of intersectionality, currently popular in feminist circles, needs to be supplemented with a resolutely historical approach, that refuses to treat the 'categories' of race, class, gender, and sexuality as if they were transparent or self-evident. We need an analysis that is both synchronic and diachronic, and we need an approach that is capable of admitting its limitations and failures. To the extent that intersectional models are subject to reification, we need to resist the tendency to allow categories which are introduced for the sake of clarity and inclusiveness to congeal into ideas that operate in a way that Jordan specifies as automatic. We need to recall the complexity of the territories that concepts such as race, class, gender, and sexuality attempt to 'capture,' to remember that in fact they constitute a messy terrain, in which the boundaries separating these 'concepts' are far from clear, where these 'concepts' bleed into one another, and mutually constitute one another, sometimes in negative and reactive ways. The lived experience of race and the phenomenon of racism have often been the invisible ground on which gender theory has played itself out. As such, they have constituted the fertile soil out of which (white) ideas have emerged, which have come to constitute prevailing feminist theories. While there is clearly no way of purifying or decontaminating feminist theory, as if one could merely subtract its racist underpinnings, and leave the rest, it is necessary for feminist theory to confront and combat its own racist history through a concerted effort that challenges the implicit or explicit racism that has become characteristic of it. This will mean contesting some ideas that have gained popularity. Following Bhattacharjee, I have suggested, for example, that the private/public distinction, which has been important to feminist thinking and strategies, has also had limited purchase when it comes to raced minorities. In order that the central organizing categories of feminism do not continue to be race-blind, we need to remain vigilant concerning the new contours of emergent forms of feminism. Whatever forms emerge, feminists need to take responsibility for their own histories and concepts, without finding new targets of discrimination on which to project our own fears, limitations, inadequacies, and blindspots.

ANNOTATED BIBLIOGRAPHY

The following bibliography interprets 'philosophy' with some latitude. Feminist theories and gender studies are inherently interdisciplinary, so that it is hard to isolate the discipline of philosophy from other disciplines when it comes to this topic. Some texts included below might not fit a narrow definition of philosophy, but nonetheless constitute important theoretical interventions.

Alexander, Jacqui and Chandra Talpade Mohanty. *Feminist Genealogies, Colonial Legacies, Democratic Futures*, ed. New York: Routledge, pp. 170–182. An excellent anthology includes a number of key articles including the following: Bhattacharjee (explores the experience of South Asian women in relation to the themes of domestic violence and work, and contests oversimplified interpretations of the public/private opposition). Guerrero (an historically informative and theoretically rigorous analysis of America's colonialist appropriation of native American land and ways of life). Hammonds (an astute analysis that explains how black women's sexuality has been rendered simultaneously invisible and hypervisible, as black women have been demonized and pathologized). Mohanty (explores the effects of globalized capital on third-world women).

Battersby, Christine. 1999. *Gender and Genius: Towards a Feminist Aesthetics*. Women's Press Ltd. One of the few feminist philosophers in England (at the University of Warwick), Battersby undertakes an examination of Kantian aesthetics, asking such questions as, why there have been no great women artists, and developing a feminine concept of genius to counter that provided by Kant.

Beauvoir, Simone de. 1953. *The Second Sex*. Trans. H. M. Parshley. New York: Alfred A. Knopf. A feminist classic: over 800 pages (even in a notoriously bad, abridged translation), covering everything from Marxism and psychoanalysis to biology and literature. Inspired by the approach of existentialist ethics, Beauvoir explores the conditions that made women the 'other' of men.

Braidotti, Rosi. 1994. *Nomadic Subjects: Embodiment and Sexual Difference in Contemporary Feminist Theory*. New York: Columbia University Press.

A nomadic subject, Braidotti is Italian, has lived in France and Australia, and teaches in the Netherlands. Influenced by Deleuze and Guattari, and by Irigaray, among others, Braidotti's work is resolutely postmodern, pluralist, interdisciplinary, and politically engaged.

Butler, Judith. 1990. *Gender Trouble: Feminism and the Subversion of Identity*. New York: Routledge. A groundbreaking work that fuses insights from philosophers such as Beauvoir, Derrida, Foucault, Lacan, and Wittig to produce an original analysis of how our gendered ideas solidify, congeal or become naturalized in ways that seduce us into thinking that culturally contingent ideas about gender are grounded in and caused by a previously existing bedrock of sex. Butler's intervention as a feminist and queer theorist is essential to understand current debates in both fields, and repays close reading, as do Butler's later works, including *Bodies that Matter*, the *Psychic Life of Power*, and *Undoing Gender*.

Chow, Rey. 1993. *Writing Diaspora: Tactics of Intervention in Contemporary Cultural Studies*. Bloomington: Indiana University Press. One of Chow's astute, well observed and important contributions to postcolonial theory, that broadens it beyond its more usual referent of South Asia.

Collins, Patricia Hill. 1991. *Black Feminist Thought: Knowledge, Consciousness, and the Politics of Empowerment*. Perspectives on Gender, vol. 2. New York: Routledge. Influenced by feminist standpoint theory, Collins exposes the systematic bias towards whiteness in mainstream feminist theory, and reclaims black feminist intellectual traditions. By writing neglected black women writers back into feminist history and theory, Collins challenges traditional, white, feminist assumptions about knowledge and truth.

Cornell, Drucilla. 1995. *The Imaginary Domain: Abortion, Pornography and Sexual Harassment*. New York: Routledge. With a background in law, Cornell's approach is informed by Derrida, Levinas, Lacan, and Rawls, among others. In a cogent and important discussion of philosophy, gender, and the law, Cornell rethinks pro-choice arguments, for example, calling for a new imaginary on which to ground our thinking of maternity. Perhaps it is no accident that it is in the sphere of legal studies that some of the most pressing theoretical issues made themselves felt before philosophy began to engage with them fully.

Deutscher, Penelope. 1997. *Yielding Gender: Feminism, Deconstruction and the History of Philosophy*. New York: Routledge. A savvy, original, smart, and clearly written discussion of gender, dealing with, among other theorists and philosophers, Beauvoir, Butler, Derrida, Irigaray, Kofman Le Doeuff, Rousseau, St Augustine and Sedgwick. The guiding thread of the book is the constitutive instability of gender. Deutscher stages a confrontation between Australian feminists of reason (including Genevieve Lloyd) and American deconstructive feminists (influenced by French theory).

Fausto-Sterling, Anne. 2000. *Sexing the Body: Gender Politics and the Construction of Sexuality*. New York: Basic Books. This is an original, important, and very readable account of how scholars, particularly biologists, construct ideas about sexuality, ideas that derive from political and moral contests over cultures and economics. While this is not strictly speaking a philosophical work – it is written for a general audience by a feminist biologist – it has important philosophical implications for the idea of gender.

Freud, Sigmund. 1953. 'Female Sexuality.' *The Standard Edition of the Complete Psychological Works.* Vol. 21. Trans. James Strachey. London: Hogarth Press and the Institute of Psycho-analysis. One of Freud's late essays dealing specifically with female sexuality, in contrast to most of his earlier work, which largely focuses on male sexuality, while occasionally adding a paragraph or two that briefly and inadequately explains how his masculinist theories might be adapted to women.

Gatens, Moira. 1996. *Imaginary Bodies: Ethics, Power and Corporeality.* London: Routledge. An important collection of essays. In particular, the opening essay, 'A critique of the sex/gender distinction,' shows how the Cartesian dichotomy between mind and body, albeit inadvertently, continues to inform the feminist distinction between gender and sex, such that gender tends to be interpreted as a voluntarist construction, while sex is aligned with the body. Other essays anticipate the later focus of Gatens' work on the importance of Deleuze and Spinoza for feminism.

Haraway, Donna J. 1991. *Simians, Cyborgs, and Women: The Reinvention of Nature.* New York: Routledge. A biologist by training, Haraway has acquired something of a cult following. More influenced by postmodernism than most feminist theorists to have engaged questions of feminism and science, her writing, which covers everything from primates and dogs to technology and philosophy, can be compelling.

hooks, bell. 2000. *Feminism is for Everybody.* London: Pluto Press. It is hard to know which of the many books that hooks has published to include – they are all worth reading – but this has such a great title that it is hard to resist. What distinguishes her writing is her ability to produce prose that is consistently politically engaged, theoretically profound, and yet accessible. Her interdisciplinarity is a plus too – she writes with insight on film, art, culture, politics, and theory.

Irigaray, Luce. 1985. *Speculum of the Other Woman.* Trans. Gillian C. Gill. Ithaca: Cornell University Press. A profound engagement with the Western tradition of philosophy and psychoanalysis, which enacts a kind of parodic mimesis, showing how women's bodies and thought have constituted the excluded ground of the Western canon and culture. Includes essays on Freud and Plato.

Lorraine, Tamsin. 1999. *Irigaray and Deleuze: Experiments in Visceral Philosophy.* Ithaca: Cornell University Press. An astute discussion exploring the affinities between Irigaray and Deleuze's thought, which I include in part because I have only begun to explore Deleuze's impact on feminist thought here, while barely touching on Irigaray.

McWhorter, Ladelle. 1999. *Bodies and Pleasures: Foucault and the Politics of Sexual Normalization.* Bloomington: Indiana University Press. Inspired by Foucault, this is a funny, wise, well-written, and very readable analysis of lesbian sexuality. It is also a wonderful resource for anyone who wants to get a handle on Foucault's mode of thinking.

Mill, J.S. 1983. *The Subjection of Women*. London: Virago. Known for his liberalism and his utilitarianism, Mill is the first male philosopher systematically to address the question of women's oppression in this 1869 essay. The influence of Harriet Jacobs Taylor on this aspect of his philosophy is not to be underestimated.

Mitchell, Juliet, and Jacqueline Rose, ed. 1982. *Jacques Lacan and the Ecole Freudienne*. Trans. Jacqueline Rose. London: Macmillan. Not only does this collection bring together most of the important works by Lacan that relate to women and sexual difference, but the two introductions are indispensable. Mitchell contextualizes psychoanalysis against the background of Marxist feminism, while Rose provides an excellent overview of Lacan and the question of women.

Narayan, Uma. 1997. *Dislocating Cultures: Identities, Traditions and Third World Feminism*. New York: Routledge. A theoretically sophisticated yet accessible intervention in feminist postcolonial theory. The opening essay, 'Contesting Cultures,' is exemplary. Narayan deftly fuses together autobiographical narrative with incisive theoretical analysis of how women's bodies often become the ground upon which competing and selective myths of Eastern and Western nationalisms are played out.

Oliver, Kelly. 2001. *Witnessing: Beyond Recognition*. Minneapolis: University of Minnesota Press. Influenced above all by Julia Kristeva in her earlier work, Oliver's more mature work develops feminist theory in a way that takes more seriously than others the question of race. This book argues for the need to go beyond a Hegelian model of recognition, based on the master/slave dialectic that still inspires a good deal of feminist theory, suggesting that we need to embrace instead a model that takes seriously the testimony of others. Oliver's work is a thorough engagement with social and political philosophy and psychoanalytic theory, which also extends to film. See also her important book, co-written with Trigo, *Noir Anxiety*, which, like *Witnessing*, takes seriously Kristeva's notion of abjection and thinks it through in relation to film noir.

Spelman, Elizabeth. 1988. *Inessential Woman: Problems of Exclusion in Feminist Thought*. Boston: Beacon Press. One of the earliest books to be written by a white feminist to make a cogent case for the need to make race central to feminist philosophy, this text includes analysis of canonical texts, such as those by Plato and Aristotle, as well as analyses of Beauvoir and Chodorow.

Spivak, Gayatri Chakravorty. 1988. 'Can the Subaltern Speak?' In *Marxism and the Interpretation of Culture*, ed. Cary Nelson and Lawrence Grossberg. Urbana: University of Illinois Press. A widely read and widely cited intervention that has set the terms for postcolonial feminist theory, which makes the important case for the need for French intellectuals such as Deleuze and Foucault to take on board the pressing questions posed by globalized capitalism. The question Spivak is concerned with is how to voice the concerns of the subaltern – the unheard, female other of postcolonial theory.

Willett, Cynthia. 1995. *Maternal Ethics and other Slave Moralities*. New York: Routledge. Taking its title from Nietzsche's analysis of bad conscience and ressentiment, this analysis seeks a third alternative to the idea of mastery and recognition which Hegel's master/slave dialectic makes central, as well as to psychoanalytic theories, by turning to African-American theorists such as Frederick Douglass, hooks, Audre Lorde, Cornel West, and Patricia Williams, grappling not only with the problem of sexual difference, but equally with the question of racial difference.

Wittig, Monique. 1992. *The Straight Mind and Other Essays*. Boston: Beacon Press. An important collection of essays, which I include in part because of its impact on Butler (one of the most important feminist/queer theorists of our time). A controversial but spirited intervention which makes the controversial but intriguing claim that the only viable way to exit the category of women is to be a lesbian.

Wollstonecraft, Mary. 1975. *A Vindication of the Rights of Women*. London: Penguin. Since this is the first readily identifiable philosophical, feminist text (written in 1791), it really has to be included. The prose style might strike modern readers as quaint and convoluted, but its interest is not limited to the historical. It also represents a very early, serious, feminist argument.

Woolf, Virginia. 1956. *Orlando: A Biography*. New York: Harcourt Brace & Company. I include this text for its fantasy quality. It is not traditional philosophy exactly, but its blend of biography, satire, and novel is profoundly philosophical and ahead of its time in so many ways, not least in its meditation on transgender. I could have equally included Woolf's literary *tour de force*, *A Room of One's Own* (but this way I mention it anyway!)

Young, Iris Marion. 1990. *Justice and the Politics of Difference*. Princeton: Princeton University Press. One of the important contributions of this book, written by a political philosopher and social theorist, is that it includes an early appropriation of Julia Kristeva's notion of abjection (developed in her book *Powers of Horror*), showing how it illuminates not only sexualized, but also racialized and classed experience, and exhibiting the fluidity of the abject. See also Young's recently revised *Throwing Like a Girl and Other Essays*, which takes its cue from, among other theorists, Merleau-Ponty.

Ziarek, Ewa Płonowska. 2001. *An Ethics of Dissensus: Feminism, Postmodernity and the Politics of Radical Democracy*. Stanford: Stanford University Press. Ziarek develops an alternative to two extremes, both of which are incapable of accepting that race and gender confine us in special ways. On the one hand there is a politics of difference that refuses to differentiate ethically between subjects, and on the other hand there is the demand for a normative conception of justice that refuses to take seriously the need for an agonistic politics. Butler, hooks, Irigaray, Kristeva, Levinas, Lyotard, Mouffe, and Spillers, among others, inform this tightly argued book.

BIBLIOGRAPHY

Ahmed, Sarah. 2005. 'The Skin of the Community: Affect and Boundary Formation.' In *Revolt, Affect, Collectivity: The unstable boundaries of Kristeva's polis.* ed. T. Chanter and E. Ziarek. Albany, New York: State University of New York

Anderson, Benedict. 1991. *Imagined Communities: Reflections on the Origin and Spread of Nationalism.* New York: Verso.

Anzaldúa, Gloria, ed. 1990. *Making Face, Making Soul: Haciendo Caras: Creative and Critical Perspectives by Women of Color.* San Francisco: Aunt Lute Foundation.

Bartky, Sandra Lee. 1990. 'Foucault, Femininity, and the Modernization of Patriarchal Power.' In *Femininity and Domination: Studies in the Phenomenology of Oppression.* New York: Routledge, pp. 63–82.

Beardsworth, Sara. 2004. *Julia Kristeva: Psychoanalysis and Modernity.* Gender Theory Series. ed. T. Chanter. Albany, New York: State University of New York.

Beauvoir, Simone de. 1953. *The Second Sex.* Trans. H. M. Parshley. New York. Alfred A. Knopf.

Benhabib, Seyla. 1992. *Situating the Self: Gender, Community and Postmodernism in Contemporary Ethics.* New York: Routledge.

Benjamin, Jessica. 1990. *The Bonds of Love: Psychoanalysis, Feminism, and the Problems of Domination.* London: Virago.

Benjamin, Walter. 1968. 'The Work of Art in the Age of Mechanical Reproduction.' In *Illuminations: Essays and reflections*, ed. Hannah Arendt. New York: Schocken Books.

Bernstein, Richard. 1983. *Beyond Objectivism and Relativism.* Philadelphia: University of Pennsylvania Press.

Bhattacharjee, Anannya. 1997. 'The Public/Private Mirage: Mapping Homes and Undomesticating Violence Work in the South Asian Immigrant Community.' In *Feminist Genealogies, Colonial Legacies, Democratic Futures*, ed. M. Jacqui Alexander and Chandra Talpade Mohanty. New York: Routledge, pp. 308–29.

Braidotti, Rosi. 2002. *Metamorphoses: Towards a Materialist Theory of Becoming.* London: Polity.

Braidotti, Rosi. 2000. 'Teratologies.' In *Deleuze and Feminist Theory*, ed. Ian Buchanan and Clare Colebrook. Edinburgh: Edinburgh University Press.

——1994. *Nomadic Subjects: Embodiment and Sexual Difference in Contemporary Feminist Theory*. New York: Columbia University Press.

——1991. *Patterns of Dissonance*. Trans. Elizabeth Guild. Cambridge: Polity.

Bray, Abigail, and Clare Colebrook. 1998. 'The Haunted Flesh: Corporeal Feminism and the Politics of (Dis)Embodiment.' *Signs*, 24 (1): 35–67.

Brennan, Teresa. 1993. *History after Lacan*. London: Routledge.

Brownmiller, Susan. 1975. *Against Our Will: Men, Women, and Rape*. New York: The Ballantine Publishing Group.

Butler, Judith. 1993. *Bodies that matter: On the Discursive Limits of 'Sex.'* New York: Routledge.

——1990. *Gender Trouble: Feminism and the Subversion of Identity*. New York: Routledge.

Calhoun, Cheshire. 1994. 'Separating Lesbian Theory from Feminist Theory'. *Ethics* 104 (April): 558–81.

Carby, Hazel. 2000. 'White Woman Listen! Black Feminism and the Boundaries of Sisterhood.' In *Theories of Race and Racism*, ed. Les Back and John Solomos. New York: Routledge, pp. 389–403.

Chanter, Tina. 1995. *Ethics of Eros: Irigaray's Rewriting of the Philosophers*. New York: Routledge.

Chodorow, Nancy. 1978. *The Reproduction of Mothering*. Berkeley: University of California Press.

Chopin, Kate. 1976. *The Awakening*, ed. Margaret Culley. Norton Critical Edition. New York: Norton.

Chow, Rey. 1999. 'The Politics of Admittance: Female Sexual Agency, Miscegenation, and the Formation of Community in Frantz Fanon.' In *Frantz Fanon: Critical Perspectives*, ed. Anthony C. Alessandrini. New York: Routledge, pp. 34–56.

——1998. *Ethics after Idealism: Theory, Culture, Ethnicity, Reading*. Bloomington and Indianapolis: Indiana University Press.

Code, Lorraine. 1993. 'Taking Subjectivity into Account.' In *Feminist Epistemologies*, ed. Linda Alcoff and Elizabeth Potter. New York: Routledge, pp. 15–48.

Colebrook, Clare. 2000. 'Introduction.' In *Deleuze and Feminist Theory*, ed. Ian Buchanan and Clare Colebrook. Edinburgh: Edinburgh University Press.

Collins, Patricia Hill. 1991. *Black Feminist Thought: Knowledge, Consciousness, and the Politics of Empowerment*. Perspectives on Gender, vol. 2. New York: Routledge.

Conley, Verena Andermatt. 2000. 'Becoming-Woman Now.' In *Deleuze and Feminist Theory*, ed. Ian Buchanan and Clare Colebrook. Edinburgh: Edinburgh University Press.

Crenshaw, Kimberlé. 1992. 'The Last Taboo,' in *Race-ing Justice, Engendering Power: Essays on Anita Hill, Clarence Thomas and the Construction of Social Reality*, ed. Toni Morrison. New York: Pantheon Books.

Davis, Angela Y. 1999. *Blues Legacies and Black Feminism: Gertrude 'Ma' Rainey, Bessie Smith and Billie Holliday*. New York: Vintage Books.

Deleuze, Gilles. 1997. *Essays: Critical and Clinical*. Trans. Daniel Smith and Michael A. Greco. Minneapolis: University of Minnesota Press.

——1995. *Negotiations, 1972–1990*. Trans. Martin Joughin. New York: Columbia University Press.

——1994. *Difference and Repetition*. Trans. Paul Patton. New York: Columbia University Press.

Deleuze, Gilles. 1992. *Expressionism in Philosophy: Spinoza*. Trans. Martin Joughin. New York: Zone Books.

——1988. *Spinoza: Practical Philosophy*. Trans. Robert Hurley. San Francisco: City Lights Books.

——1983. *Nietzsche and Philosophy*. Trans. Hugh Tomlinson. London: The Athlone Press.

Deleuze, Gilles, and Félix Guatarri. 1994. *What is Philosophy?* Trans. Hugh Tomlinson and Graham Burchill. New York: Columbia University Press.

——1988. *A Thousand Plateaus: Capitalism and Schizophrenia*. Trans. Brian Massumi. Minneapolis: University of Minnesota Press.

Deleuze, Gilles, and Michel Foucault. 1977. 'Intellectuals and Power. A Conversation between Michel Foucault and Gilles Deleuze.' In *Foucault, Language, Counter-Memory, Practice: Selected Essays and Interviews*. Trans. Donald F. Bouchard and Sherry Simon. Ithaca: Cornell University Press.

Deleuze, Gilles, and Clare Parnet. 2002. *Dialogues II*. Trans. Hugh Tomlinson and Barbara Habberjam. New York: Columbia University Press.

Delphy, Christine. 1993. 'Rethinking Sex and Gender.' *Women's Studies International Forum*. Vol. 16, no. 1: 1–9.

Derrida, Jacques. 1997. 'Choreographies: Interview with Christie McDonald.' In *Feminist Interpretations of Jacques Derrida*, ed. Nancy J. Holland. Re-reading the Canon series, ed. Nancy Tuana. University Park: Pennsylvania University Press.

——1982. *Margins of Philosophy*. Trans. Alan Bass. Chicago: Chicago University Press; *Marges de la philosophie*. Paris: Minuit, 1972.

——1981a. *Dissemination*. Trans. Barbara Johnson. Chicago: University of Chicago Press.

——1981a. *Positions*. Trans. Alan Bass. Chicago: University of Chicago Press.

——1976. *Of Grammatology*. Trans. Gayatri Chakravorty Spivak. Baltimore and London: The Johns Hopkins University Press; *De la grammatologie*. Paris: Minuit, 1967.

Descartes, René. 1979. *The Philosophical Works of Descartes*. Vol. 1. Trans. Elizabeth S. Haldane and G.R.T. Ross. Cambridge: Cambridge University Press.

Diprose, Rosalyn. 1994. *The Bodies of Women: Ethics, Embodiment and Sexual Difference*. New York: Routledge.

Douglas, Mary. 1999. *Purity and Danger: An analysis of the concepts of pollution and taboo*. New York: Routledge.

Engels, Friedrich. 1985. *The Origin of the Family, Private Property and the State*. Harmondsworth, Middlesex: Penguin Books.

Fanon, Frantz. 1968. *The Wretched of the Earth*. Trans. Constance Farrington. New York: Grove Press.

——1967. *Black Skin, White Masks*. Trans. Charles Lam Markmann. New York: Grove Press.

Feder, Ellen K. and Emily Zakin. 1997. 'Flirting with the Truth: Derrida's discourse with "woman" and wenches.' In *Derrida and Feminism: Recasting the Question of Woman*, ed. Ellen K. Feder, Mary C. Rawlinson, and Emily Zakin. New York: Routledge.

Ferrell, Robyn. 1991. 'The Passion of the Signifier and the Body in Theory.' *Hypatia* 6 (3): 172–84.

Feyerabend, Paul. 1975. *Against Method: Outline of an Anarchistic Theory of Knowledge*. London: New Left Books.

Fire (Canada/India, 1996). Deepa Mehta, 104 min., Trial by Fire Films, Inc.

Firestone, Shulamith. 1972. *The Dialectic of Sex: The Case for Feminist Revolution*. New York: Bantam Books.

Flax, Jane. 1986. 'Gender as a Social Problem: In and For Feminist Theory.' *American Studies/Amerika Studien, Journal of the German Association for American Studies*.

Flieger, Jerry Aline. 2000. 'Becoming-Woman: Deleuze, Schreber and Molecular Identification.' In *Deleuze and Feminist Theory*, ed. Ian Buchanan and Clare Colebrook. Edinburgh: Edinburgh University Press.

Foucault, Michel. 1977. *Discipline and Punish: The Birth of the Prison*. Trans. Alan Sheridan. New York: Vintage Books.

——1972. *The Archaeology of Knowledge and the Discourse on Language*. Trans. A. M. Sheridan Smith. New York: Pantheon Books.

Freud, Sigmund. 1953. 'Beyond the Pleasure Principle.' *The Standard Edition of the Complete Psychological Works*. Trans. James Strachey. Vol. 18. London: Hogarth Press and the Institute of Psycho-analysis.

Gairola, Rahul. 2002. 'Burning with Shame: Desire and South Asian Patriarchy, from Gayatri Spivak's "Can the subaltern speak?" to Deepa Mehta's *Fire*.' *Comparative Literature* 54 (4) Fall: 307–24.

Gandhi, Leela. 1998. *Postcolonial Theory: A Critical Introduction*. New York: Columbia University Press.

Gatens, Moira. 2000. 'Feminism as "Password:" Re-thinking the Possible with Spinoza and Deleuze.' *Hypatia*. 15 (2): 59–75.

——1996. *Imaginary Bodies: Ethics, Power and Corporeality*. New York: Routledge.

Gatens, Moira, and Genevieve Lloyd. 1999. *Collective Imaginings: Spinoza, Past and Present*. New York: Routledge.

Gilligan, Carol. 1982. *In a Different Voice: Psychological Theory and Women's Development*. Cambridge, Massachusetts: Harvard University Press.

Goldberg, David Theo, ed. 1990. *Anatomy of Racism*. Minneapolis: University of Minnesota Press.

Goswami, Namita, and Tina Chanter. 2006. Joint presentation on Deepa Mehta's *Fire*, DePaul University, Chicago, 28 March.

Goulimari, Pelagia. 1999. 'A Minoritarian Feminism? Things to Do with Deleuze and Guattari.' *Hypatia*. 14 (2).

Gramsci, Antonio. 1971. *Selections from Prison Notebooks*, ed. and trans. Quinton Hoare and Geoffrey Nowell Smith. New York: International Publishers.

Grant, Judith. 1987. 'I Feel Therefore I Am: A Critique of Female Experience as a Basis for Feminist Epistemology.' *Women and Politics* 7 (3): 99–114.

Grosz, Elizabeth. 1997. 'Ontology and Equivocation: Derrida's Politics of Sexual Difference.' In *Feminist Interpretations of Jacques Derrida*, ed. Nancy J. Holland. Re-reading the Canon series, ed. Nancy Tuana. University Park: Pennsylvania University Press.

Grosz, Elizabeth. 1994. *Volatile Bodies: Toward a Corporeal Feminism*. Bloomington: Indiana University Press.

Guerrero, Marie Anna Jaimes. 1997. 'Civil rights versus sovereignty: Native American women in life and land struggles.' In *Feminist Genealogies, Colonial Legacies, Democratic Futures*, ed. Jacqui Alexander and Chandra Mohanty. New York: Routledge.

Guha, Ranajit, and Gayatri Chakravorty Spivak, eds. 1988. *Selected Subaltern Studies*. New York: Oxford University Press.

Guillaumin, Colette. 1999. ' "I know it's not nice, but . . . " The changing face of "Race." ' In *Race, Identity, and Citizenship: A Reader*, ed. Rodolfo D. Torres, Louis F. Mirón and Jonathan Xavier Inda. Oxford: Basil Blackwell, pp. 39–46.

Halperin, David. 1990. *One Hundred Years of Homosexuality and other Essays on Greek Love*. New York: Routledge.

Hammonds, Evelynn M. 1997. 'Toward a Genealogy of Black Female Sexuality: The Problematic of Silence.' In *Feminist Genealogies, Colonial Legacies, Democratic Futures*, ed. Jacqui Alexander and Chandra Mohanty, New York: Routledge, pp. 170–82.

Harasym, Sarah, ed. 1990. *The Post-Colonial Critic: Interviews, Strategies, Dialogues*. With Gayatri Chakravorty Spivak. New York: Routledge.

Haraway, Donna. 2003. 'Situated Knowledges: The Science Question in Feminism and the Privilege of Partial Perspective.' In *Feminist Theory Reader: Local and Global Perspectives*, ed. Carole McCann and Seung-Kyung Kim. New York: Routledge. Reprinted from *Feminist Studies*, vol. 14, no. 3 (Spring 1988): 575–99.

——1991. *Simians, Cyborgs, and Women: The Reinvention of Nature*. New York: Routledge.

Harding, Sandra. 1993. 'Rethinking Standpoint Epistemology: "What is Strong Objectivity"?' In *Feminist Epistemology*, ed. Linda Alcoff and Elizabeth Potter. New York: Routledge, pp. 49–82.

——1991. *Whose Science? Whose Knowledge?* Ithaca, New York: Cornell University Press.

——1986. *The Science Question in Feminism*. Ithaca: Cornell University Press.

Hartmann, Heidi. 1981. 'The Unhappy Marriage of Marxism and Feminism.' In *Women and Revolution: A discussion of the unhappy marriage of Marxism and feminism*, ed. Lydia Sargent. Boston: South End Press.

Hawkesworth, Mary E. 1989. 'Knowers, Knowing, Known: Feminist Theory and Claims of Truth.' In *Feminist Theory in Practice and Process*, eds. Micheline R. Malson, et al. Chicago: University of Chicago Press, pp. 327–51.

Hegel, G. W. F. 1977. *The Phenomenology of Spirit*. Trans. A. V. Miller. Oxford: Clarendon Press.

hooks, bell. 1984. *Feminist Theory: From Margin to Center*. Boston: South End Press.

Hull, Gloria T., Patricia Bell Scott, and Barbara Smith. 1982. *All the Women are White, All the Blacks Are Men, But Some of Us Are Brave: Black Women's Studies*. New York: The Feminist Press.

Irigaray, Luce. 1993. *An Ethics of Sexual Difference*. Trans. Carolyn Burke and Gillian C. Gill. Ithaca, New York: Cornell University Press.

——1985. *Speculum of the other woman*. Trans. Gillian C. Gill. Ithaca, New York: Cornell University Press.

——1985. *This Sex Which Is Not One*. Trans. Catherine Porter and Carolyn Burke. Ithaca, New York: Cornell University Press.

Jordan, June. 2003. *Some of Us Did Not Die. New and Selected Essays of June Jordan*. New York: Basic/Civitas Books.

Kerber, Linda K., Catherine G. Greeno, Eleanor E. Maccoby, Zella Luria, Carol B. Stack, and Carol Gilligan. 1986. 'On *In a Different Voice*: An Interdisciplinary Forum.' *Signs: Journal of Women in Culture and Society* 11 (2): 304–33.

Khalidi, Ramla and Judith Tucker. 1996. *Arab Women: Between Defiance and Restraint*, ed. Saabagh, Suha. New York: Olive Branch Press.

Kittay, Eva, and Diana Meyers. 1987. *Women and Moral Theory*. Rowman and Littlefield.

Klein, Melanie. 1986. *The Selected Melanie Klein*, ed. Juliet Mitchell. New York: The Free Press.

Kristeva, Julia. 1987. *Tales of Love*. Trans. Leon S. Roudiez. New York: Columbia University Press.

——1986. 'Women's Time.' In *The Kristeva Reader*, ed. Toril Moi. Oxford: Basil Blackwell.

——1984. *Revolution in Poetic Language*. Trans. Margaret Waller. New York: Columbia University Press.

——1982. *Powers of Horror: An essay on abjection*. Trans. Leon S. Roudiez. New York: Columbia University Press.

——1977. *About Chinese Women*. Trans. Anita Barrows. New York: Urizen Books.

Lacan, Jacques. 1977. *Ecrits: A selection*. Trans. Alan Sheridan. London: Tavistock Publications.

Landry, Donna, and Gerald Maclean, eds. 1996. *The Spivak Reader: Selected Works of Gayatri Chakravorty Spivak*. New York: Routledge.

Laqueur, Thomas. 1990. *Making Sex: Body and Gender from the Greeks to Freud*. Cambridge, Massachusetts: Harvard University Press.

Lennon, Kathleen, and Margaret Whitford, eds. 1994. *Knowing the Difference: Feminist Perspectives in Epistemology*, London: Routledge.

Levinas, Emmanuel. 1987. *Time and the Other* [and additional essays]. Trans. Richard A. Cohen. Pittsburgh, Pennsylvania: Duquesne University Press.

Lim Y. C., Linda. 1983. 'Capitalism, Imperialism, and Patriarchy: The dilemma of third-world women workers in multinational companies.' In *Women, Men and the International Division of Labor*, ed. June C. Nash and Maria P. Fernandez-Kelly. Albany, New York: State University of New York Press.

Locke, John. 1924. *Two Treatises of Government*. London: J.M. Dent & Sons.

Lorraine, Tamsin. 1999. *Irigaray and Deleuze: Experiments in Visceral Philosophy*. Ithaca: Cornell University Press.

——2003. 'Living a time out of joint.' In *Between Deleuze and Derrida*, ed. Paul Patton and John Protevi. London: Continuum.

Ma vie en rose [My life in pink] (Belgium, 1997). Alain Berliner, 89 min. Sony Pictures.

Margaret's Museum (Canada, 1995). Mort Ransen, 118 min. Cinépix Film Properties Inc.

McClintock, Anne. 1995. *Imperial Leather: Race, Gender and Sexuality in the Colonial Contest*. New York: Routledge.

Mclane, Janice. 2003. 'Starving for Power: Websites as Public Anorexia.' Conference Presentation at the State University of New York. Celebrating Thirty Years of Stony Brook Philosophy Doctorates, October 8–11, 2003.

Mead, Margaret. 1935. *Sex and Temperament in Three Primitive Societies*. New York: William Morrow.

Mehta, Deepa. http://www.Zeitgeistfilms.com/films/fire/presskit.pdf. Last accessed 5.5.06.

Mickey Mouse goes to Haiti: Walt Disney and the Science of Exploitation. 1996. National Labor Committee. Crowning Rooster Arts.

Mill, J. S. 1983. *The Subjection of Women*. London: Virago.

Minow, Martha. 1991. 'Feminist Reason: Getting It and Losing It' [1988]. In *Feminist Legal Theory: Readings in Law and Gender*, ed. Katharine T. Bartlett and Rosanne Kennedy. Boulder: Westview Press, pp. 357–69.

Mohanty, Chandra Talpade. 1997. 'Women Workers and Capitalist Scripts: Ideologies of domination, common interests, and the politics of solidarity.' In *Feminist Genealogies, Colonial Legacies, Democratic futures*, ed. Jacqui Alexander and Chandra Mohanty. New York: Routledge.

——1991. 'Under Western Eyes: Feminist Scholarship and Colonial Discourses.' In *Third World Women and the Politics of Feminism*, ed. Chandra Mohanty, Ann Russo, and Lourdes Torres. Bloomington: Indiana University Press.

Morrison, Toni. 1993. *The Bluest Eye*. New York: Alfred A. Knopf.

Mouffe, Chantal. 1993. *The Return of the Political*. London: Verso.

Mullarkey, John. 1997. 'Deleuze and Materialism: One or Several Matters?' *South Atlantic Quarterly. A Deleuzian Century?* Special issue, ed. Ian Buchanan, 96 (3): 440–63.

Murray Li, Tania. 2003. '*Masyarakat Adat*, Difference and the Limits of Recognition in Indonesia's Forest Zone.' In *Race, Nature and the Politics of Difference*, ed. Donald S. Moore, Jake Kosek, and Anand Pandian. Durham and London: Duke University Press.

Nagel, Thomas. 1989. *The View from Nowhere*. Oxford: Oxford University Press.

Narayan, Uma. 1997. *Dislocating Cultures: Identities, Traditions and Third World Feminism*. New York: Routledge.

——1989. 'The Project of Feminist Epistemology: Perspectives from a Nonwestern Feminist.' In *Gender/Body/Knowledge: Feminist Reconstructions of Being and Knowing*, ed. Alison Jaggar and Susan R. Bordo. New Brunswick and London: Rutgers University Press.

Nietzsche, Friedrich. 1989. *On the Genealogy of Morals*. Trans. Walter Kaufmann and R. J. Hollingdale. *Ecce Homo*. Trans Walter Kaufmann. New York: Vintage Books.

——1968. *The Twilight of the Idols*. Trans. R. J. Hollingdale. Harmondsworth, Middlesex: Penguin Books.

Noddings, Nel. 1984. *Caring: A Feminine Approach to Ethics and Moral Education*. Los Angeles: University of California Press.

Oakley, Ann. 1972. *Sex, Gender and Society*. New York: Harper & Row.

Oliver, Kelly. 2001. *Witnessing: Beyond Recognition*. Minneapolis: University of Minnesota Press.

Oliver, Kelly and Benigno Trigo. 2003. *Noir Anxiety*. Minneapolis: University of Minnesota Press.

Olkowski, Dorothea. 2000. 'Body, Knowledge and Becoming-Woman: Morpho-logic in Deleuze and Irigaray.' In *Deleuze and Feminist Theory*, ed. Ian Buchanan and Clare Colebrook. Edinburgh: Edinburgh University Press.

Orlando. (U.K. 1992). Sally Potter. 92 mins. Sony Pictures Classics.

Pateman, Carole. 1988. *The Sexual Contract*. Stanford, California: Stanford University Press.

Patton, Paul. 2000. *Deleuze and the Political*. Thinking the Political Series, eds. Keith Ansell-Pearson and Simon Critchley. London and New York.

Plato. 1978. *Republic*. Plato in twelve volumes. Vols 5–6. Trans. Paul Shorey. The Loeb Classical Library. Cambridge, Massachusetts: Harvard University Press.

——1975. *Lysis, Symposium, Gorgias*. Plato in twelve volumes. Vol. 3. Trans. W. R. M. Lamb. The Loeb Classical Library. Cambridge, Massachusetts: Harvard University Press.

Putnam, Hilary. 1981. *Reason, Truth, and History*. Cambridge: Cambridge University Press.

Rhode, Deborah L. 1991. 'Feminist Critical Theories.' In *Feminist Legal Theory: Readings in Law and Gender*, ed. Katharine T. Bartlett and Rosanne Kennedy. Boulder: Westview Press, pp. 333–50.

Roelofs, Monique. 2004. 'The Aesthetics of Ignorance.' Paper presented at the Ethics and Epistemologies of Ignorance Conference, Penn State University, 24–25 March.

Rorty, Richard. 1994. *Objectivity, Relativism, and Truth*. Philosophical Papers, vol. 1. Cambridge: Cambridge University Press.

——1986. *Philosophy and the Mirror of Nature*. Oxford: Basil Blackwell.

Rubin, Gayle. 1975. 'The Traffic in Women: notes on the "political economy" of sex.' In *Toward an Anthropology of Women*, ed. Rayna R. Reiter. New York: Monthly Review Press.

Ruddick, Sara. 1980. 'Maternal Thinking.' *Feminist Studies* 6 (2) Summer: 342–67.

Russo, Vito. 1989. *The Celluloid Closet: Homosexuality in the Movies.* New York: Harper & Row.

Scott, Joan W. 1988. 'Deconstructing Equality vs. Difference. or, The Uses of Poststructuralist Theory for Feminism.' *Feminist Studies* 14 (1) Spring: 32–50.

Secomb, Linnell. 1999. 'Beauvoir's Minoritarian Philosophy.' *Hypatia.* 14 (4): 96–113.

Setz, Margaret. 2001. 'Wartime sexual violence against women: a feminist response. In Legacies of the Comfort Women of World War II', ed. Margaret Setz and Bonnie B. C. Oh. Armonk, NY: M. E. Sharpe Inc.

Spelman, Elizabeth. 1988. *Inessential Woman: Problems of Exclusion in Feminist Thought.* Boston: Beacon Press.

Spillers, Hortense. 1997. 'All the things you could be by now if Sigmund Freud's wife was your mother.' In *Female Subjects in Black and White. Race, Psychoanalysis, Feminism,* ed. Elizabeth Abel, Helen Moglen, and Barbara Christian. Berkeley: University of California Press.

Spinoza, Benedict de. 1955. *On the Improvement of the Understanding, The Ethics, Correspondence.* Trans. R. H. M. Elwes. New York: Dover Publications.

Spivak, Gayatri Chakravorty. 1999. *A Critique of Postcolonial Reason: Toward a History of the Vanishing Present.* Cambridge, Massachusetts: Harvard University Press.

——1988. 'Can the Subaltern Speak?' In *Marxism and the Interpretation of Culture,* ed. Cary Nelson and Lawrence Grossberg. Urbana: University of Illinois Press.

——1987. *In Other Worlds: Essays in Cultural Politics.* London and New York: Methuen.

Sunstein, Cass R., ed. 1990. *Feminism and Political Theory.* Chicago: University of Chicago Press.

Weate, Jeremy. 2001. 'Fanon, Merleau-Ponty and the Difference of Phenomenology.' In *Race: Blackwell Readings in Continental Philosophy,* ed. Robert Bernasconi, Oxford: Blackwell. pp. 169–183.

Winch, Peter. 1958. *The Idea of a Social Science and its Relation to Philosophy.* London: Routledge and Kegan Paul.

Wittig, Monique. 1992. *The Straight Mind and Other Essays.* Boston: Beacon Press.

Wollstonecraft, Mary. 1975. *A Vindication of the Rights of Women.* London: Penguin.

Woolf, Virginia. 1956. *Orlando: A Biography.* New York: Harcourt Brace & Company.

Young, Iris Marion. 2005. *On Female Body Experience: 'Throwing Like a Girl' and Other Essays.* Oxford: Oxford University Press.

——1997. *Intersecting Voices: Dilemmas of Gender, Political Philosophy, and Policy.* Princeton University Press.

——1990. *Justice and the Politics of Difference.* Princeton, New Jersey: Princeton University Press.

Young, Lola. 2000. 'Imperial Culture: The Primitive, the Savage and White Civilization.' In *Theories of Race and Racism*, ed. Les Back and John Solomos. London: Routledge, pp. 267–86.

Zita. Jacqueline. 1998. 'Male Lesbians and the Postmodernist Body.' *Body Talk: Philosophical Reflections on Sex and Gender*. New York: Columbia University Press, pp. 85–108.

INDEX

Index compiled with the help of Heather Rakes.